TO LIFE!

Also by Harold Kushner in EasyRead Type

WHO NEEDS GOD

TO LIFE!

A Celebration of
Jewish Being
and Thinking

Harold Kushner

WALKER AND COMPANY
New York

Library of Congress Cataloging-in-Publication Data
Kushner, Harold S.
     To life!: a celebration of Jewish being and thinking / Harold Kushner /
—1st large print ed.
        p.   cm.
ISBN 0-8027-2680-1 (lg. print)
1. Judaism—Essence, genius, nature. 2. Judaism—Doctrines. 3. Spiritual life—Judaism. 4. Jewish way of life. 5. Large type books. I. Title.
BM565.K78   1994
296—dc20   94-21190
                                                                       CIP

Andre Ungar's Alternate Version of the Weekday Amidah from *Siddur Sim Shalom*, edited, with translations, by Rabbi Jules Harlow. Published by the Rabbinical Assembly and the United Synagogue of America. Copyright © 1985 by the Rabbinical Assembly. Reprinted by permission.

First Large Print Edition, 1994
Walker and Company
435 Hudson Street
New York, New York 10014

Printed in the United States of America

10 9 8 7 6 5 4 3 2 1

To Ariel and Isaac Haber
who promise me immortality

Contents

Acknowledgments

*T*HE SPIRITS of many people inhabit this book, and I am grateful to all of them. Professor Franklin Littell first suggested that I write it. James H. Silberman was my editor, as he has been for past collaborations. He had a clear vision of what this book should be, and kept me focused on it. Only he and I know how much better this book is for his suggestions and insights. My agent, Peter Ginsberg, was the matchmaker for this venture, as he has been for others. My wife, Suzette, was a constant source of encouragement, and deserves more credit than these words convey. All of my teachers, from the men and women who taught me the Hebrew alphabet when I was seven years old to my professors in graduate school at the Jewish Theological Seminary, have left their mark on my mind and heart and thus upon this book. And a final word of appreciation to the late Howard Nelson who, twenty years ago, invited me to join an ecumenical panel on Boston's leading radio station and share my ideas with a large and varied audience. After our first show, he said to us, "You've just spoken to more people than St. Paul did in his whole life."

May this book enrich your soul as they have enriched mine.

To Life!

*T*o LIFE—these two words represent so much of what Judaism is about. They suggest first that Judaism is about how to live, not just what to believe. They convey an optimistic attitude toward life, investing our energy in living rather than in worrying about dying, asking us to enjoy the pleasures of this life rather than noticing all the things that are wrong with it, emphasizing life in this world rather than pinning our hopes on finding satisfaction in some world to come. As the traditional Jewish toast over a glass of wine, *To life* conveys a sense of exuberance, a readiness to enjoy the pleasures of this world. It removes from wine, and from other pleasures, the taint of sin and self-indulgence, and invites us to look at all that God has created and find it good. The sages teach us that "in time to come, everyone will have to account for all the good things God created which he refused to enjoy."

Does any other people celebrate the special moments of life, the births and birthdays and weddings, with as much food, as much laughter and as many tears, as Jews do? This book offers you an introduction to the forms and customs, the joys and consolations of Judaism. It can be the door to life.

TO LIFE!

1

Life Is the Question, Judaism Is the Answer

*T*HIS IS a book about Judaism, a four-thousand-year-old tradition with ideas about what it means to be human and how to make the world a holy place. Judaism goes back beyond Buddha, beyond Confucius. Its notions of God and life were the sources of Christianity and Islam. Yet despite its age, perhaps because essential human nature hasn't changed that much over the centuries, because issues of life and death, parents and children, human hopes and human failures remain constant over the generations even as the surrounding landscape changes, the ideas of Judaism are important to us today. Anyone who takes his or her destiny as a human being seriously has to be acquainted with these ideas.

This is a book about the Jewish people. From the visions of the biblical prophets and the poetry of the Psalms to the theories of Einstein and Freud, from the custom of measuring time in weeks to the polio vaccine and a dozen other major medical discoveries, this tiny sliver of the human race has influenced our world (and inspired more irrational fear and hatred) than any group its size.

But mostly, this is a book about life, how to understand what it means to be authentically human and how to respond to that challenge. The question to which it addresses itself is not "How [or why] should I be Jewish?" but "How can I be truly human?" Judaism is not the problem. Life is the problem, and Judaism is the answer. It can teach you how to find the hidden rewards of holiness in the world, and how to cope with its uncertainties and disappointments. A prominent literary critic once said, "Being Jewish is the easiest way to be a human being."

That is what this book is about. Who are you, the reader, and who am I, the author? You may be a Jew whose Jewish education was largely confined to the years of your childhood. There were so many things your teachers wanted to tell you then but could not, partly because we had so little time and partly because even if you could have asked the serious questions back then, you probably weren't ready to hear the answers. Though there is much in Jewish life that children can enjoy and be thrilled by, and though children can read and respond to biblical tales, the real stuff of

Judaism is a system of great power and subtlety. It is meant to be confronted by adults, not children. Becoming Bar Mitzvah at age thirteen was meant to begin, not to conclude, the process of learning what it means to be a Jew. For you, then, this book will tell you all the things you never learned in Hebrew School. It will continue the conversation that was abandoned years ago, but this time on an adult level.

You may have come away from your childhood exposure to Jewish learning with the impression that Judaism was a collection of irrelevant customs and unconnected prohibitions stemming from its origins in ancient times. You may have gotten the impression from the popular culture—from movies and television programs—that Jewish religion was something old-fashioned and ill suited to the modern world, a subject of humor or a source of conflict between parents and children, between boyfriend and girlfriend. You may be a Jewish woman who grew up in an age when people believed girls didn't need to learn about Judaism. You may have seen your brothers going to Hebrew School and becoming Bar Mitzvah and felt yourself excluded from the whole enterprise. You may be a self-proclaimed secular Jew, a bearer of a Jewish name and sense of Jewish identity, aware that your name and identity may make you a target of antisemites, too proud to give up your Jewishness for that reason yet unconvinced that the label stands for anything you could take seriously. Or perhaps you have just come to a point in your life when you find yourself musing that "there must be more to life than this." Wherever you may be coming from, I will try to show you the relevance, the coherence, and the importance of those fragments of Judaism you have picked up along the way, how they fit together to make sense and speak to us today. But more than that, I will try to go beyond making sense and show you how these customs open the door to passion, to holiness, to a deepening of life's joys and a fearless confrontation with its sorrows. I will try to help you understand, as you may never have understood, why your ancestors considered these ideas worth living by and worth dying for.

Some years ago, my wife and I were vacationing in Nepal in the shadow of the Himalayas. There our group was joined by a young Jewish man named Bill, who had just completed a six-month stay at a Buddhist monastery. Bill was a soul questing for spiritual meaning. I asked him what he was looking for in Nepal that he had never been able to find in Judaism, and he recited the familiar complaints about the superficiality of his home and Hebrew School upbringing. (My wife's comment was that if Bill had been born a

Buddhist, at age thirty-five he might have entered a yeshiva.)

I spent a lot of time talking to Bill on that trip, trying to show him how he could find in Judaism the spiritual depth and seriousness he had been looking for around the world, without having to uproot his soul from its Jewish origins. I ran into Bill recently when I was lecturing in the city where he lives. He told me that he is active in the local Jewish federation, that he volunteers at a nursing home, and that he is continuing to study Judaism. If you are at all like Bill, I hope this book will do for you what our conversations did for him.

You may be a person of whatever religious affiliation or no formal affiliation at all, who wants to know more about Jews and Judaism. You may want to understand more deeply the religious background of the conflict in the Middle East. You may have Jewish friends and coworkers who invite you to share their holidays and family celebrations. Increasingly in the late twentieth century, you may have a Jewish daughter-in-law and Jewish grandchildren, and you may feel the need to know more about their tradition.

Or you, the reader, may be a committed Christian who has come to realize that you cannot fully understand your own faith without understanding the Jewish roots from which it grew. You may know that Jesus was born and lived as an observant Jew, that all the apostles and most of his early followers were Jews, that the Christmas story can only be understood against the background of an oppressed Jewish people longing for the promised Messiah of the House of David, and that the account of the Crucifixion is a retelling of the original Passover story. As one professor of theology puts it, "He who knows only one religion doesn't really know any." Moreover, at a time when the forces of paganism and secularism are so prominent in American life, you may have come to realize that Jews and Christians need to see beyond their differences, significant though they may be, and rediscover the heritage we have in common. Though I myself am a committed Jew and not a Christian, one of my purposes in writing this book is to enrich your Christian commitment, not to challenge it.

I have written this book for the person who grew up Jewish but never learned what it was about, and for the person who never grew up with a Jewish identity but now has a serious interest in Judaism. I have written it to convey to you both the clarity and the passion of Jewish life.

And who am I? In addition to being somebody's husband and somebody's father, in addition to being a fan of folk music and the Boston Red Sox, I have been a rabbi for more than thirty years, most of them in a suburban community west of Boston. As a rabbi, I have taught my congregants about the Jewish tradition and called on its wisdom and spiritual resources to help them in their time of need, whether the need was bereavement, unemployment, divorce, or problems with growing children. Then, at age forty-six, having written a book I felt compelled to write about how we coped with a family tragedy, I unexpectedly found myself an author with a national audience for what I had been teaching my suburban congregation, connecting the traditional wisdom of Judaism to the quests and concerns of modern men and women.

I have written three books in that vein. This is the fourth. It is a very personal book, Judaism as I have come to understand it, live it, and teach it. Another rabbi would have written a different book, emphasizing different things, explaining some things differently, and including things I may have left out. (I hope this is not the only Jewish book you will ever read.)

This leads me to what I would call Rule One: Any time we ask a question "What does Judaism say about . . . ? ," the only correct answer will always begin: "Some Jews believe as follows, and other Jews believe something different." The reason for this is not just that we are a highly individualistic, independent-minded people. The main reason is that we have never found it necessary to spell out exactly what we are supposed to believe. With no precise definition of what Judaism believes, you would expect the result to be chaos and anarchy, but it's not, because Jewish identity is not centered in belief. It is centered in community and history. We can tolerate great diversity of theological opinion, in part because nobody can be completely sure he or she is right about the nature of God, heaven and hell, and other theological matters, but mostly because Jews have something that binds us together beyond, and more effectively than, common belief.

One of the most important differences between Judaism and Christianity is that we were a people before we had a religion. Christianity begins with an idea—the incarnation of God in Jesus, the crucifixion and resurrection of Jesus as a way of redeeming man from sin. If a person believes that idea, he is a Christian. If he doesn't share that belief, however liberally or metaphorically he may understand it, one might question whether he is in fact a Christian. Ultimately, Christians form communities, but the faith-commitment is always primary. That is what they have in common. That is what makes them Christians.

But Judaism begins not with an idea but with a community, the great-great-grandchildren of Abraham, Isaac, and Jacob, going through the experience of Egyptian slavery and miraculous liberation from slavery. Out of that shared experience and the subsequent encounter with God at Mount Sinai, we shaped a religion—holy days and rituals to celebrate the formative events of our history, prayers and Scriptures to spell out how we understand our relationship to God. But throughout it all, it is the participation in the community that defines us as Jews; the creeds and rituals are secondary.

I remember the first day of a course in rabbinical school called Philosophies of Religion. The professor, Mordecai Kaplan, asked us all to write down the names of the ten greatest Jews of the twentieth century. We listed Einstein, Freud, Theodore Herzl, and other scientists, statesmen, and writers. When we were done, he said, "Now, next to each name, list the synagogue he attended each week." The point was that virtually none of them was a regular synagogue-goer. Yet they were all clearly Jewish. They thought of themselves as Jewish, the world saw them as Jewish, rabbinical students considered them the greatest Jews of the century. But they were not Jewish by virtue of their religious observance. They were Jewish through their devotion to the Jewish people and community.

The implications of this difference in emphasis between Jews and Christians are major. For one thing, it means that you are born a Jew in a way that you cannot be born a Christian. The child of Christian parents is born a pagan and must be baptized in order to become a Christian. In some traditions, that choice can be made only when the child becomes an adult. But the child of a Jewish mother is automatically a Jew because he or she is part of that historical community. He does not have to become Jewish through a ceremony any more than he needs a ceremony to make him the child of his parents.

In the Roman Catholic Church, the ultimate punishment, the worst thing the Church can do to a person, is excommunication, cutting him off from communion, breaking his church-mediated relationship to God. Judaism, too, has a form of excommunication (though it hasn't been used seriously since the days of Spinoza in the seventeenth century). But in Judaism, excommunication does not cut you off from God. It separates you not from communion but from community. The reprobate Jew who has been excommunicated can pray to God every morning and every evening if he wishes, but none of his Jewish neighbors will talk to him, buy from him, or sell to him. (In the modern world, this is all hypothetical. Whenever I have heard of an attempted excommunication, it was by some fringe group and not taken seriously by anyone else.) The excommunicated Jew can pray to God alone, at home or elsewhere, but if he comes to synagogue, he will not be counted toward the *minyan,* the quorum of ten required to conduct a public service. If the essence of religious identity is not your beliefs about God but your membership in a God-seeking community, then the ultimate heresy is not to deny the existence or attributes of God but to deny your obligations to the people around you, and the most severe punishment is not to cut you off from God (can any human being do that to another?), but to cut you off from the surrounding community. (Is it only because I am Jewish that I find that a more dreadful prospect?)

These are the reasons why Judaism can tolerate so much diversity of belief. If I may stretch a metaphor, being Jewish is like being part of a family, while being a Christian is more like belonging to an organization that exists for a specific purpose. In such a group, people who are strangers to each other are brought together by their shared beliefs and goals, and that sharing of belief is what they have in common. When you find you no longer share the beliefs of the other members of the organization, and you can't convince them to see things your way, you consider leaving to join, or even form, another organization for people who see things the way you do. But in a family, there may be people with whom you have very little in common—you may be a political liberal and your uncle a staunch conservative; you enjoy Mozart and Vivaldi while your cousin is into heavy metal—but you feel bound to them by family ties. You may not like each other, you may not agree with each other, but you know that you belong to each other.

(Though it may seem surprising to those who have grown up in an American-European culture shaped by Christianity, most world religions grew out of a community, a people, rather than an idea. No other world religion, except perhaps some strands of Buddhism, places the emphasis on belief and theology that Christianity does.)

This difference in emphasis may help us understand the phenomenon of Jews who feel very strongly and proudly Jewish but have never thought seriously about what they believe about God and may go for months at a time without uttering a prayer or performing a religious ritual. It may shed light on the readiness of American Jews not only to respond generously to American charitable causes, but to work on behalf of Jews in foreign lands whom they don't know and will probably never meet. Judaism is less about believing and more about belonging. It is less about what we owe God and more about what we owe each other, because we believe God cares more about how we treat each other than He does about our theology.

*   *   *

The story is told of Dr. Chaim Weizmann, the chemist who became the first president of modern Israel, at a time when he was lobbying British politicians to win their support for the Zionist effort to gain a Jewish homeland. One member of the House of Lords said to him, "Why do you Jews insist on Palestine when there are so many undeveloped countries you could settle in more conveniently?" Weizmann answered, "That is like my asking you why you drove twenty miles to visit your mother last Sunday when there are so many old ladies living on your street."

We love Israel not because it is perfect, but because it is ours. We love our parents not because they are better parents than anyone else has, but because they are *our* parents. They gave us life and nurtured us. And we love Judaism not because we have examined its theological postulates and found them compelling and valid, but because it is ours. It is the community through which we learn how to be human and how to share life with the people around us.

But if Judaism is about belonging, about learning to be part of a community, it is not only about that. It is about being part of a very special community, a community made special by its relationship to God. And it is to the story of that relationship that we now turn.

2

The Stories We Tell
About Ourselves

---

*H*ERE IS the story we tell about ourselves, to help us understand who we are, who God is, and what we and God expect of each other.

In the beginning, God created an orderly world out of the chaos and darkness that preceded Creation. God separated the light from the darkness, the dry land from the waters. God populated the world with plants and trees, birds, fish, and animals, and gave them all the capacity to reproduce themselves, so that tomato plants would bear tomatoes and cats would bear kittens. It was a perfect, stable, orderly, completely predictable world.

But God, who includes within Himself the capacity for goodness, for happiness, and for moral choice as well as for stability and perfection, felt that something was missing from this perfect and predictable world. Because everything was programmed, there could be no choice.

All living creatures would do what their instincts impelled them to do. Especially there could be no *moral* choice, no choosing right over wrong, good over bad. And so, perhaps because God loves goodness even more than He loves perfection, God said *to the animals* that He had just created in the previous verse, "Let us make a human being in our image, yours and Mine. Let us together create a being who will be an animal in some ways, needing to eat, to sleep, to procreate, but will resemble Me in some ways, being aware of moral distinctions in a way that no other living creature is."

God created Adam and Eve, a higher order of being than any creatures that had existed before them, as exemplified by their power to name (and classify) the other animals. He blessed them with the capacity to be moral, to obey Him not out of fear of punishment, but on the basis of free choice. To give them the opportunity to display their moral qualities, God gave them one commandment: You may eat any of the plants, and the fruit of any of the trees in the garden, except the fruit of one tree alone. Had Adam and Eve been able to obey that single rule, they would have added to the world the one thing that it lacked, the one thing that God Himself could not create: goodness, freely choosing to do what is right. God's world would have been complete.

But Adam and Eve disobeyed God. They ate the forbidden fruit. Their descendants were even worse. Cain was a murderer, as was his great-great-grandson Lamech. People became more and more violent and corrupt, until finally, after ten generations of moral degeneration, God felt He had to do something about it. He sent a flood to wash the world clean of the stain of human corruption, sparing only the one righteous man He found, Noah, and his family. After the flood, God gave Noah a few basic rules (against murder, theft, incest, and cruelty) and told him to start over again, repopulating the world.

But Noah, too, disappointed God. Perhaps overwhelmed by the prospect of rebuilding a destroyed world, Noah planted a vineyard and got drunk. His sons quarreled among themselves, their descendants came into conflict, and by the tenth generation after the flood, things were as bad as they ever were.

At this point, God decided to change His tactics. He had come to realize that maybe He was expecting too much of human beings, asking them to be moral in the midst of an immoral community. Human beings are weak. Goodness and self-control do not come easily to us. We are too easily influenced by the examples of people around us. Instead of looking for one man (Adam, Noah) who would be strong enough to stand up to his environment, God would fashion an environment, an entire community of people who were trying to be good, in the hope that they would support and sustain each other, and bring out the best in each other.

God chose Abraham, a man who showed some innate gift for moral sensitivity, and instead of summoning him to be better than his neighbors, God summoned him to be the founder of a special people. His descendants would know that they had a special relationship with God. They would go through the experiences of slavery and liberation, so that the saving power of God would be real, not only theoretical, in their lives and so that they would always feel a special kinship with the enslaved and oppressed. As the Bible would repeatedly instruct the Israelites, "You shall deal kindly with the stranger, for you were strangers in the land of Egypt and you know the heart of the stranger."

The rest of the Book of Genesis, the first book of the Bible, is the story of Abraham's family, of how future generations came to terms with God's call, and of how, by the book's end, that family had grown to a good-sized clan and had migrated to Egypt at a time of famine.

The second biblical book, Exodus, is the hinge on which all of Jewish history turns. The world inhabited by Abraham's descendants at the end of Exodus is totally different from the one on which the curtain goes up at the book's beginning. If Genesis is the basic biblical statement about what God wants and needs from human beings in general, Exodus is the definitive statement about God's relationship to the Jewish people. It tells the story of how an anonymous band of slaves was transformed into the nation that taught the human race about God.

In Exodus, we read of how the Egyptian Pharaoh reduced his Hebrew subjects to slavery and set them to work building royal storehouses. We read of how the Hebrew people cried out to God in their misery, and how God intervened on the side of the downtrodden, summoning Moses to confront Pharaoh, afflicting the Egyptians with plagues, each more terrible than the one before it, until finally Pharaoh relented and let the people go.

Seven weeks after their liberation from slavery, the Israelites found themselves at the foot of Mount Sinai where, in a moment that changed the course of history for the Jewish people and the world forever, they met God. It was here that God proclaimed the Ten Commandments and Moses spent forty days on the mountaintop receiving the Tablets of the Law. Before Mount Sinai, there had been laws against murder, theft, adultery, and other violations of the public order, but they had always been cast in terms of "if . . .

then . . ." If your ox damages your neighbor's property, then you are responsible for repairing it. If you kill your neighbor's slave, then he can take, or kill, your slave to get even. But at Mount Sinai, for what seems to be the first time in recorded human history, rules were laid down not on the basis of what is legal or illegal, but on the basis of absolute right and wrong: Thou shalt not! Murder and adultery are not only against the law; they are fundamentally wrong, and will remain wrong even if people try to change the law.

But the point of the Ten Commandments is not simply that they spoke in terms of an absolute morality rather than a social consensus. Equally important is that they were delivered to an entire people. God invites the entire Israelite people to join with Him in a Covenant, a contract. The Israelites promise to live a distinctive, moral, God-centered life, and God for His part promises to bless the people with His presence, give them a homeland of their own, and protect them there.

The idea behind the Covenant seems to be this: Only the rare individual can live by a moral code significantly different, and significantly more demanding, than the one by which his neighbors live. Put the average honest man into a business setting where most of his colleagues lie to make a sale and pad their expense accounts to augment their salaries, and it will be very hard for him to remain honest. Send a bright young person to a college where his or her best friends spend their time drinking instead of studying, and chances are that his or her education will suffer. So instead of asking individuals to rise above their society, God sets out to create a community where ordinary people, not saints, would reinforce each other's efforts to do the right thing. If God's aim is to make His world complete by having people freely choose to do what is good and right, instead of looking for the unique individual, the saint, the virtuous hero, a Noah or an Abraham, He would create a model society, where doing good will not be a heroic choice but just the way people do things.

As we tell the story, what was communicated at Sinai was more than the Ten Commandments. After God had addressed the people, inviting them to join Him in a Covenant, Moses remained alone with God on the mountaintop for forty days and forty nights, as God spelled out for him how this model people should behave in the smallest details of their lives, from what they should eat and wear to how they should treat convicted criminals and captured prisoners of war, from instructions about worshipping Him with animal offerings to warnings about ridding their community of astrologers and fortune-tellers.

God had given Adam and Eve just one commandment, thinking that if they just kept that one, they would be totally obedient. The flaw in that reasoning was that, by breaking that one rule, the only one they had to live by, they were totally disobedient. They were doing nothing right. At Sinai, God decided that the Israelites, with a desire for morality but no natural instinct for it, needed more explicit instructions. The biblical record of what God told Moses to tell the Israelites is known as the Torah, and refers to the first five books of what we call the Bible (or the Hebrew Bible) and what Christians call the Old Testament, the books that contain the stories leading up to Mount Sinai and the rules for living we were given there: Genesis, Exodus, Leviticus, Numbers, Deuteronomy. While we regard the entire Hebrew Bible as holy and treat it with reverence, the Torah is given a special, higher degree of holiness.

The word *Torah* is often translated "Law," but this is a not entirely accurate, and in fact somewhat misleading, translation. There are laws in the Book of Exodus and in Deuteronomy, telling us how to deal with thieves, kidnappers, and murderers. But most of the contents cannot really be described as legal. A better translation for *Torah* would be "the Teaching." The word *Torah* comes from the same root as the Hebrew word for teacher and guide, one who shows the way.

Perhaps the most important word in the Torah, after the name of God, is the word *brith,* usually translated as *covenant.* Unfortunately, *covenant* is almost as foreign and unfamiliar a term as *brith,* so it requires some explanation. A covenant is like a contract, an agreement in which two parties make commitments to each other. It can be between two equal parties, as in a typical business deal, an agreement to buy a house or a car, for example, spelling out what the two parties can expect of each other. But in the ancient Near East, a covenant would more likely be between two unequal parties, perhaps between a powerful king and a community that agreed to serve him, and it would spell out their respective obligations.

The immense importance of seeing the revelation of Sinai as the forming of a Covenant, and the Torah as the record of that Covenant, is that it proclaims the idea that God and Man have obligations to each other. We owe God something, the obligation to discern and choose the good, in exchange for His giving us life, health, food to eat, and people to love us. No longer is our relationship to God like that of an infant to a parent, expecting to be fed and clothed and comforted simply because we need it and cry for it. At Sinai, God said to the Jewish people, "You are grown up enough so that I expect you to earn your keep, to do something in exchange for all I do for you." And the idea of a Covenant articulates the idea that we can expect things from God, that He will not be an arbitrary ruler. The world may not always be fair, and God may not be able to protect us from the consequences of natural law and human cruelty, but it will be a stable world, with predictable sunrises and sunsets, a world in which the laws of chemistry and physics will be the same tomorrow as they were yesterday.

What does God get out of the agreement? He gets the one thing He cannot do for the world Himself, the phenomenon of people freely choosing to be good. And what is in it for us, the Jewish people? Our reward will be the sense of God's presence, the feeling that we are doing something for God and entering into a specially close relationship with Him in the process. When the prophets want to threaten the Israelite people with the worst punishment they can imagine, they warn them that God will remove His presence from their midst and turn them back into an ordinary people again.

The second half of the Book of Exodus, after the Revelation of the Torah at Sinai, begins to spell out the ways in which a Jew is called on to live a God-oriented life, including ethical obligations (if you take a poor man's coat as security for a loan, you have to give it back to him at night when it gets cold; Exodus 22:25), ritual obligations (don't cook meat and milk together; Exodus 34:26), and civil and criminal laws (if your animal damages your neighbor's field, you have to compensate him from the best of your harvest; Exodus 22:4). It then spends several chapters on details for building the Tabernacle, a portable shrine to house the Tablets of the Ten Commandments and be a focus for Israelite worship.

The Book of Exodus, spelling out our relationship to God and our obligations to Him under the terms of the Covenant, contains the basic elements of Jewish life and thought:

—the story of how God intervened to redeem a group of slaves, Abraham's descendants, and give them freedom;

—the account of God's summoning Israel to enter into a Covenant with Him at Mount Sinai;

—the idea that human beings can be like God in their ability to take ordinary moments and make them holy, and along with that, the concept of the sacred deed, the *mitzvah,* as a unique way of sanctifying an otherwise profane world and thereby making God's world complete;

—the notion of sacred time, days that would be different from other days, days in which we would disengage ourselves from our ordinary pursuits and remind ourselves of who we were summoned to be;

—the notion of sacred space, a return to Sinai as it were, a place set aside for us to go to in order to meet God, to worship God, to be cleansed and strengthened by that encounter and to prepare ourselves to carry some of the holiness of that encounter back into the world;

—and the divine promise to give the Jewish people a home of their own, a showcase for the God-oriented life we were called on to live.

These fundamental ideas of Exodus provide the table of contents for our discussion of Judaism: the memory of redemption from slavery, the concept of the Covenant, the notion of sacred deeds, sacred days, and sacred places, and the promise of a homeland.

Not only the second half of Exodus, but the rest of the Bible and virtually everything that has been written about Judaism since biblical times (including, I suppose, this book), is an attempt to answer the question: How do you hold on to the feeling of standing before God at Sinai? When our ancestors stood at the foot of the mountain, they knew they were in the presence of God. They were inspired to be committed, generous, and loyal. But you cannot spend your whole life at the mountain. Sooner or later, you have to return to the real, everyday world with all the conflicts and compromises that entails. How do you keep alive the memory of Sinai? How do you hold on to the sense of standing before God? Exodus's answer, Judaism's answer, is that you do it with special deeds and with sacred times and places. Three thousand years of scholarship and history are a commentary on that notion.

A few pages ago, I used a verb that some readers may have found puzzling or provocative. I wrote that "God *chose* Abraham." When we are first introduced to Abraham in chapters 11 and 12 of the Book of Genesis, when God summons him to leave his home and go forth to found a new nation and be a blessing to the world, we don't know anything about him. We are not even told, as we were about Noah, that he was more righteous than his contemporaries. This choice seems to be totally arbitrary. When God speaks to Abraham's descendants at Sinai, He tells them that if they follow the ways He is setting out for them, they will be a "chosen people," His own special treasure.

The idea of the Jews as "God's chosen people" has been a highly problematical one. At the theoretical level, it offends our notion that all humans are created equal and that God loves us all equally. At the practical level, it has inspired countless episodes of Jewish neurosis and self-expectation, and of gentile resentment and envy. (Did you know that the first time the word *sin* appears in the Bible, it refers not to Adam and

Eve eating the forbidden fruit, but to Cain's resentment of Abel because God seemed to "choose" Abel and prefer him to Cain?)

What are we to make of this controversial, uncomfortable, and provocative claim that God has chosen the Jewish people to have a special relationship with Him? One professor of mine at seminary (Mordecai Kaplan, to whom I referred in the opening chapter) was so bothered by the antidemocratic, chauvinistic implications of the idea that he suggested we eliminate it from contemporary belief, putting it in the same category as the biblical suggestion that the earth is flat or that people used to live for six hundred or nine hundred years. Not venturing to rewrite the Bible, he rewrote the Jewish prayer book to eliminate all references to this notion that had caused so many ideological and social problems.

The Bible's own answer comes at two levels. First, the Bible tells us that God's love for Abraham and for the Jewish people is, like all love, irrational. It cannot be logically explained or understood. God has at least the same right that we do to fall in love with someone and leave others wondering what He sees in her. In fact, at one point the Book of Deuteronomy, summarizing Israel's history to that point, describes God as having this special relationship with the people Israel not because they were so numerous or impressive (the Torah continually describes the Israelites as being a terribly ordinary bunch, despite the extraordinary events they had lived through), but simply because He had loved their ancestors and maintained that fondness for Abraham's children.

But between the lines, another understanding of "chosenness" emerges. In summoning Israel to be a model community, so that God's goal of people choosing righteousness can be attained, God not only has in mind that the Israelites will sustain each other. He wants them to be an example to other nations. God understands that most people learn from living examples better than they learn from books. We learn to drive, to swim, to throw a football, or to play the piano not by reading a book about how to do it, but by watching people do it correctly and trying to imitate them. God does not simply want one nation acting righteously in an immoral world. It is not enough for Him that someone somewhere is choosing good over evil. God has implanted in every man and woman the potential to be human, to see beyond instinct and choose the good. The Jewish people were to be a "pilot project," a demonstration community. God would give them explicit instructions about how to carry on the God-centered life. If they did it, they would not only please God and feel good about themselves. They would bring the other peoples of the world to see how satisfying it is to live that way. Nations that had not stood at Sinai and received the Torah (though perhaps they had experienced God by going through their own enslavement and liberation) would learn from this living example. The ultimate vision of the Torah is not that the whole world will become Jewish, but that the whole world will be brought to recognize that the God worshipped by the Jews is the only true God, and that to follow his ways is to live as human beings were meant to live.

What does it mean for us as Jews to consider ourselves a "chosen people"? It certainly does not mean that we think we are better than other people, either individually or collectively. I was a congregational rabbi for thirty years, dealing professionally with Jewish families, and if there is one thing I know beyond the shadow of any doubt, it is that Jews are just as flawed, just as average, just as imperfect as everyone else. There is no claim of Jewish biological superiority. How could there be, with so much converting in and out of Judaism? We have no way of knowing how many of today's Jews are the pure biological descendants of Abraham and Sarah, though we are all their spiritual descendants.

I take the claim that the Jews are a chosen people to be not a moral or a biological statement, but a historical one. Jews today may be a lot like everybody else. Jews in ancient times may have been a lot like everybody else. But it is a historical fact that the Jews, and no one else, gave the world the Bible. It is a historical fact that the Jews introduced to the pagan world the idea of a God who demanded righteousness. It is an undisputable historical fact that the Psalms were written by Jews, and that the prophets were Jews. Even most of the books of the New Testament were written by Jews.

How did it happen that this tiny people, historically insignificant in economic, scientific, or military terms, has shaped the way the world thinks about God? I don't know, and neither does anybody else. I can offer plausible sociological explanations for why there are so many Jewish doctors and college professors (and so few Jewish professional football players), but I can't explain why the Jews of biblical times understood what God wanted of people better than anyone else did.

Some scholars have attributed it to the experience of slavery and liberation, which gave rise to a sense of obligation to repay God for His intervention. But other people escaped from slavery without going on to write the Bible. Others try to explain it on the basis of the Israelites living in the desert, which inspired them to meditate on the meaning and purpose of life because there were so few distractions on the horizon. But there were many other desert-dwelling tribes at that time, and they wrote no psalms and produced no prophets. There seems to be no rational explanation. Perhaps we can do no better than accept the Torah's own explanation of how it came into being. God, for reasons of His own, chose to make the Jewish people the instrument of His self-revelation to the world.

That does not mean that God loved (or loves) Jews more than He loves other people, only that He loves us differently. The Bible repeatedly speaks of Israel as "God's firstborn." Any of you who are parents of more than one child know that it is possible to love all of your children equally but differently, and to fasten on one of them (often the firstborn) hopes for achievement that you don't necessarily have for that child's brothers or sisters.

Sometimes the firstborn responds to these expectations with pride and responsibility, but sometimes with resentment, and usually with a mixture of both. For every younger brother who whines, "How come he gets to do things I can't do?" there may be an older brother complaining, "How come I have to do things you don't make them do?" (I am a firstborn son, so I know how the process works.) The historical circumstance of being chosen to be the bearers of God's word, of having been the first people to understand and know God, has led to a great deal of Jewish pride and achievement and to a great deal of guilt, resentment, and feelings of inadequacy. (It's not easy going around with the feeling that you have disappointed God and your family by being ordinary.)

Perhaps the most enduring issue in Jewish history is the tension between proudly accepting God's challenge to be a special people and wistfully wishing for the freedom to be normal, "like all the other nations." (In the Bible, there is no more withering put-down of Israelite behavior than to condemn it as a way of wanting to be "like all the other nations.") When the modern state of Israel was founded in 1948, half of its founders said, "This is our opportunity to be a light unto the nations, to respond to God's challenge by being an example of justice and enlightenment," while the others said, "The Swiss, the Norwegians, and the Indonesians exist without having to justify their existence by being special; this is our chance to shed the burden of specialness and become a normal people at last." In the same way, when there are social problems of poverty or prejudice in the United States, half the members of my congregation would say, "As Jews, we have a special responsibility to do something about this," while the other half would say, "All I want to do is pay my bills and raise my kids; let somebody else solve America's problems." If you are confused and ambivalent about the claim that we somehow have a special relationship to God because we are Jewish, take my word for it that ambivalence is the traditional Jewish response.

What actually happened at Sinai on that day that changed the world? Had you been there, would you actually have been able to record God's voice uttering the Ten Commandments?

Some Jews (here comes Rule One again) would insist that, yes, God actually spoke the Ten Commandments to the assembled throng, and for the next six weeks dictated the remainder of the Torah to Moses. Others would say that descriptions of God speaking are a metaphor, an attempt to put into words the extraordinary event of Revelation. How do we learn things? they would ask. Sometimes we learn by having someone tell us something directly. But sometimes an idea pops into our head by a process we don't understand, without a word being spoken. We don't know where it came from, where it was before we thought of it, or how it got into our mind, but all of a sudden it's there. The Revelation at Sinai, they would tell us, happened that way.

Martin Buber, the great Jewish theologian

who taught that all of life is rooted in relationships, suggested that sometimes we understand something just by meeting someone, without having to be told. There are some people in whose presence we find ourselves incapable of telling a lie or an off-color joke. We meet someone who has overcome a severe physical handicap, and without his or her saying anything to us, we feel differently about our own physical problems. A person coming into the presence of a great spiritual leader may come to realize the shallowness of some of his own behavior. A father looking down on his newborn child gets a message about responsibility and immortality in a way that he never understood them before. He gets that message without any words being spoken. Buber suggests that at Sinai, the Israelites came into the presence of God in an intense, immediate way and, as a result of that meeting, understood how human beings are meant to live, with a clarity that they had never had before.

The discussion of what actually happened at Sinai raises the question of how we regard the Bible. How literally do we take it? Can parts of it be true and the Word of God, if other parts of it are not? How can we even ask what happened at Sinai, when the nineteenth and twentieth chapters of Exodus purport to tell us precisely what happened there?

It is hard to give a simple answer to that question. The Bible is not a single book. It is an anthology of some two dozen books, written over a period of perhaps a thousand years. Some statements (that King Solomon built a Temple in Jerusalem and that three hundred fifty years later the Babylonians destroyed it) are undoubtedly true. Others (that the prophet Elisha helped a poor widow pay her debts by giving her a magic bottle of oil that never stopped pouring) are undoubtedly the sorts of legends that have attached themselves to prominent figures in every society. While many Orthodox Jews would accept the notion that God literally created the world in one hundred forty-four hours, others would take that story as a picturesque, memorable way of telling us something more important about our world than how long it took to come into being, something about its being a good, orderly, self-regulating place in which human beings are qualitatively different from other living creatures. In a phrase, we take it seriously but not literally.

While some may see the Torah, the first five books of the Bible, as the stenographic record of what God said to Moses on the mountaintop (not only written down accurately but copied accurately by hand for thousands of years before there were printing presses), others of us would see the Torah as an effort by inspired human beings to put into words the nature and content of their inspiration. You probably know what it feels like to try to put into words the most intense experiences of your life—to try to tell someone what it feels like to fall in love, to have a baby, to survive a near-fatal accident. You know the frustration of realizing that the words, however articulate, capture most but not all of what you are trying to convey. The Torah is the effort of inspired human beings to say, "We have met God and, as a result, we have to live our lives differently."

The first thing we need to say about the Jewish view of the Bible is that we see it as *our* book. It is not only Holy Scriptures; it is our family album. The stories of Abraham, Isaac, and Jacob are not just folk tales or Sunday School lessons. They are stories about our grandparents. The list of places at which the Israelites camped on the way to the Promised Land ("They traveled from Marah and came to Elim . . . and they traveled from Elim and came to the Red Sea" [Numbers 33:9-10]) is not just a page of trivia to be skipped by the impatient reader. It is like coming across a box of postcards sent to us by relatives on their travels. The Bible will mean more to the Jewish reader than to even the most devout Christian because it is the book his relatives wrote.

The second thing we believe about the Bible is that it is true. It is true even when it is inaccurate, because there are many ways of being true. When I was a boy, movie theaters would show a newsreel and a cartoon before the main feature. At one level, the newsreel (typically political speeches, beauty contests, and new car debuts) was true and the feature film was fiction. But at another level, if the movie was a good one, it was truer than the newsreel, because it said something true and valid about the human spirit (how different people respond to a crisis, how people are changed by love) while the newsreel did not. Shakespeare's plays are true at that level, because they portray human beings accurately and perceptively, even if people by those names never lived and never spoke the words Shakespeare puts in their mouths. And the Bible is truer than Shakespeare. No document ever written has understood the needs of the human soul as has the Bible. No other book has the power to change society, to make people say, "I may not want to hear that, but it's right."

And the third thing to be said about the Jewish view of the Bible is that Jews don't read the Bible the way one reads a novel, for the plot. You don't read it to see how it ends (though recently there have been a number of good books analyzing the Bible as literature and finding evidence of great literary skill in its pages). Nor do you read it like a newspaper or a magazine article, skimming it to get the general idea. As a contemporary scholar has put it, Jews read the Bible the way a person reads a love letter. When you read a love letter, you don't just read it for content. You try to squeeze every last little bit of meaning out of it. (Why did he sign it "Yours" instead of "Love"? Why a dash instead of a comma?)

If the Bible is "true" as a moral guide, what are we to make of biblical passages that offend our contemporary moral sensibilities, passages that seem to praise murder and bloodshed or assign women to an inferior social role? Some of the problematic passages, first of all, are the result of a misunderstanding of the text, part of the problem of trying to understand the nuances of a book written three thousand years ago, not only in a different language but in a different culture. "An eye for an eye, a tooth for a tooth," for example, is not a prescription for vengeance and mutilation, as it is so often taken to be. I can't imagine it was ever meant to be taken literally. Biblical society abhorred mutilation as a desecration of the divine image in every one of us. It understood that hurting a person deliberately was different from injuring him accidentally. It realized that the loss of an eye would mean more to one person than it would to another. And it went to great lengths to quell the desire for revenge, not to encourage it. (For example, a man who inadvertently caused the death of another was required to move to another city, so that the relatives of the deceased would not be tempted to take revenge on him when they encountered him.) "An eye for an eye" is the Bible's vivid way of saying that a person who causes harm should be punished appropriately for what he did. His punishment should be precisely what he deserves, neither more (a life for an eye) nor less (a scolding for an eye). It is a call for justice, not vengeance.

Other troubling passages reflect the society in which, and for which, the Bible was written. One hundred fifty years ago, clergymen on both sides of the slavery issue appealed to the Bible to bolster their arguments. They were both able to cite Scripture because the same Bible that teaches the dignity of all human beings also countenances people owning slaves. The reason, it would seem, is that in biblical times people who had debts and no money would sell themselves into temporary slavery to work off their debts. (Think of Jacob, unable to come up with a dowry to buy himself a wife, offering to work for his father-in-law for seven years instead.) The Bible has laws about slaves, not to *endorse* slave-owning but to *regulate* it. Similarly, because the Bible was written in a time of frequent and bloody wars, it (like the American history books on which I was raised) celebrates the victories in those wars as the working out of God's plan, not just the triumph of the mightier army. I would like to think that those bloodcurdling commands to wipe out the enemy were not God's instructions before the battle, but a retroactive way of interpreting what in fact happened as being God's will. As a professor of mine once said, "History is lived forward but understood backward." After it happened, the story was told as the playing out of God's command. And because women had no public role in biblical times, the stories and legal institutions of the Bible reflect (but certainly do not recommend) the inferior status of women.*

* Some contemporary feminists, appalled by the traditional way in which women have been treated in Western society, blame Judaism and the Bible for imposing a patriarchal system on the paganism of the Canaanites and its cult of the goddess. I think their blame is misplaced. Canaanite paganism was one of the most male-chauvinist, antifemale societies known to history. The name of the chief Canaanite deity, Baal, means simultaneously "husband" and "owner." In its verbal form, it refers to the male dimension of the sexual act. Baal-worship was a fertility cult, and the purpose of the gods was to make the harvest bountiful and the women pregnant every year. If pagans worshipped goddesses, it was not to celebrate their full humanity but to respond to their fecundity, their ability to bear children, as attested to by statuettes of goddesses that have been found, emphasizing their wombs and breasts. (When *Playboy* magazine emphasizes those parts of a woman, we correctly see it as dehumanizing.

I vividly recall a debate during my student days between two of my professors at seminary on the question of what to do when biblically based Jewish law seems to ask us to do something immoral. The first, the more liberal of the two, began by saying that God's word should never be the cause of immoral behavior. If the law seems to lead to an immoral end, we should appeal to a higher law and feel free to amend or reject it. His colleague, the more conservative, said that if you do that, you are making a human standard (how we feel about a law) superior to God's standard (what the Bible says). The liberal professor replied that, when he was morally offended by a law, it was not a matter of setting his taste against God's. Where did he learn to be morally offended by laws that treat women or foreigners as less worthy than other people? Not from secular human society, but from the pages of the Bible, which commands us to see all

Shouldn't we recognize ancient fertility cults as doing the same thing?) It seems to me that open-minded feminists should see the Bible not as the herald of patriarchal society, but as the advocate of a new way of looking at women, seeing them, perhaps for the first time in human history, as full human beings, fashioned in the image of a God who transcends gender, rather than limiting their identity to the role of sex partners and mothers.

human beings, male or female, Jew or gentile, bond or free, as bearers of God's image.

But perhaps the most important question we can ask about the Jewish attitude toward the Bible is this: What sort of people are we because of the stories we tell about ourselves, stories preserved and immortalized in the Bible? We are a people who take life in this world seriously. There is a whole spectrum of opinions among Jews as to what life will be like in the World to Come. (Since nobody can know for sure, multiple opinions flourish.) But the danger of believing too fervently in a World to Come is that you may come to care less about the imperfections of this world. So what if there is rampant crime and disease? So what if widows and other poor people are taken advantage of by the rich and powerful? This world is only God's waiting room. In Eternity, people will get what they deserve and the last shall be first.

Almost universally, Jews reject that perspective. Our creed would seem to be that God so loved this world that He lavished upon it immense care in creating it, making it an orderly, beautiful, precious place. And if we love God, we should feel obliged to treat with love the world He loves so much. I can remember one of my teachers, Abraham Joshua Heschel, telling us that Plato and Aristotle would have laughed at the prophet Isaiah. How petty to be concerned about one widow being cheated, one poor man starving. Worry instead about the *idea* of justice, the *definition* of equality, they would have told him. But the reader of the Bible is told that the abstract concept of justice is meaningless unless it is translated into the lives of every citizen.

It may be that my perspective is distorted by thirty years of officiating at the life-cycle events in Jewish families, but it is my impression that we Jews celebrate the events of this life more than other people do, perhaps because we invest more of our belief in this world and rely less on a World to Come. Do other people fuss as much about the birth of a baby, or over a child's coming of age, as we do? And while you may catch some Jews saying it, it's really not a Jewish attitude to say of a person who has died that "she is with God now." The Jewish view would be to say, "When she was alive, she was with God, and now that she has died, she is missing from God's world."

What sort of people are we because of the Bible stories we tell about ourselves? I believe there is a straight line from the biblical story of the Exodus to contemporary Jewish involvement in issues of social justice. Remembering, and annually repeating, the story of slavery and liberation, we have developed a sense of empathy for the oppressed. In a museum exhibit on the relationship between Jews and blacks, I found the following quotation from a woman named Sabrina Virgo:

> "When I was young, I was taught that being Jewish meant:
> you don't cross picket lines,
> you work for peace,
> you fight for social justice,
> you never forget the suffering of your people as a link to the suffering of others."

In Milton Himmelfarb's provocative phrase, American Jews are "the only ethnic group who earn like Episcopalians and vote like Puerto Ricans." We tend not to vote our own self-interest (middle-class Jews are more likely than other middle-class Americans to vote for higher taxes on themselves to help the poor). We tend not to vote for Jewish candidates, or for the most pro-Israel candidate. Jewish voters tend to support the candidate who seems most committed to making the world a better place.

In the early part of the twentieth century, many Jews were attracted to the Communist party not only because it replaced a cruel, viciously antisemitic czar in Russia, and certainly not because Jews are by nature revolutionaries, but because it promised to make the world better. When communism turned out to be a "god that failed," when Stalin's Russia turned out to be as brutal and as antisemitic as any czarist regime, they withdrew their loyalty. But they continued to look for a cause to follow, because they believed that the purpose of human beings on earth was to do for God the one thing He could not do for Himself, to crown His creation with goodness, and make this world, not some other far-off world, the Kingdom of God.

We learn two lessons from the stories we tell about ourselves: that God *loves* us and that God *needs* us.

God shows His love for us by reaching down to bridge the immense gap between Him and us. He shows His love for us by inviting us to enter into a Covenant with Him, and by sharing with us His precious Torah. The idea that giving us laws is a sign of God's love is one of the fundamental theological differences between Judaism and Christianity. Saint Paul in the New Testament sees the Law as a snare and a trap. Having laws he cannot live up to is what makes him a sinner. Laws are seen as the instrument of a harsh, restrictive, punishing God, and need to be superseded by the rule of love and forgiveness. Judaism—while admiring love and forgiveness every bit as much as does Saint Paul (who, by the way, was Jewish)—sees the role of Law totally differently. In our view, a loving parent does not show his or her love by telling a child, "Do whatever you want, and I will still love you." That is not love but an abdication of responsibility. A loving parent says to a child, "I care very much about you, and although I cannot live your life for you, I want you to have the benefit of my experience." Jews have understood from the beginning that ours was a religion of love because it did not leave us to find our way through life unaided. It offered advice, insight, and guidelines.

The claim that God needs us is not so much a statement about God as it is about us. We are called on to do something for God and for the world. We are important; we are empowered. The foundation story of Judaism teaches us these two lessons. It is our obligation to be a role model for all nations, showing them what the God-oriented life looks like, and it is our obligation to make God's world complete by giving Him the one thing He cannot do for Himself, by freely choosing to do good. God depends on us to complete and sanctify His world, and we disappoint Him cosmically if we fail to respond to His challenge.

3

The Sacred Deed—
Making the Ordinary
Extraordinary

WHILE MANY OF US tend to see the world as divided into the holy (the realm of the religious) and the profane (the ordinary, nonreligious, meaning everything else; the word *profane* literally means outside or in front of the church), theologian Martin Buber taught that the division is really between the holy and the not-yet-holy. Everything in God's world can be holy if you realize its potential holiness. One of the fundamental teachings of Judaism is that the search for holiness, for the encounter with God, is not confined to the synagogue. Everything we do can be transformed into a Sinai experience, an encounter with the sacred. The goal of Judaism is not to teach us how to escape from the profane world to the cleansing presence of God, but to teach us how to bring God into the world, how to take the ordinary and make it holy.

To review succinctly some of the points made in the last chapter:

Why did God create human beings? So that they could contribute the one thing His creation lacked, the act of freely choosing goodness.

What makes human beings different from other living creatures? We have eaten of the fruit of the Tree of the Knowledge of Good and Evil. Where other creatures can be obedient or disobedient, only human beings can be *good.*

How can we exercise our humanity in the direction of goodness? By freely choosing to do what God would have us do, instead of following our instincts as all other animals do.

We tend to think of laws as restricting our freedom. ''That would be a perfect parking place but it's illegal.'' ''We could save a lot of money doing that, but it's against the law, so we can't.'' We think of freedom as meaning being unencumbered by laws, free to go where we want, to do what we want, to touch the museum exhibit without hindrance. But Judaism insists that living by God's laws is a matter not only of obedience, but of a more important kind of freedom.

It may seem strange to speak of the Torah, with its myriad regulations and prohibitions, as a source of freedom. If a non-Jewish friend and I go into a restaurant together, and he can choose any item from a menu offering beef, pork, and shellfish, while I can ask only for a boiled egg or a tuna sandwich because I observe the Jewish dietary laws, what sense does it make to say that I am freer than he is? The freedom the Law offers is the freedom of the athlete who disciplines his body so that he is free to do things physically that you and I are incapable of. It is the freedom of being the master of appetite rather than its slave. I once gave a sermon at a Passover service in which I referred to the message of Passover as "From Slavery to Freedom." A member of my congregation, a professional musician who teaches at Harvard, told me afterward that he always took the message to be *"Through* Slavery to Freedom." It is only by subjecting oneself to rigorous discipline, as the musician or the athlete does, that we gain the ability to do demanding and impressive things. When my congregant was young, he had to practice scales and finger exercises while his friends were outdoors playing ball, and there were times when he resented it. But because he practiced, he is now free to play a Beethoven sonata well enough to move an audience with its beauty.

So many of the rules and rituals of the Jewish way of life are spiritual calisthenics, designed to teach us to control the most basic instincts of our lives—hunger, sex, anger, acquisitiveness, and so on. We are not directed to deny or stifle them, but to control them, to rule them rather than let them rule us, and to sanctify them by dedicating our living of them to God's purposes. The freedom the Torah offers us is the freedom to say no to appetite.

Think of it this way: There may come a time in your life when your future happiness will depend on your being able to say no to something tempting: a shady business deal, a compromise of your principles, an illicit sexual adventure. If you have had virtually no experience saying no, if the message from parents and salesmen has consistently been "If you want it, we can work something out," what are the chances of your acting properly at that moment? And what are your chances for happiness? But if all your life you have practiced the control of instinct, saying no to food, to sexual opportunities, to other temptations, how much better will your chances be?

I once appeared on a cable television show to debate my theology of tragedy with a professor of theology from a Baptist seminary in the Southwest. He defined his position as believing in the inerrancy of Scripture, that every word of the Bible was of God, and he chided me for being selective as to which verses I would accept as of divine origin. I responded by asking him, "In that case, how come you eat pork chops and I don't,

when the eleventh chapter of Leviticus specifically forbids it and you believe that those are
God's words?" He answered, "Because I believe
that our Lord Jesus Christ came to liberate us
from the ritual commandments and left only the
ethical ones as binding." I challenged him again:
"Even if that were the case, why do you define
the dietary laws of Leviticus as ritual, not ethical? What is a more important ethical issue in
today's world than teaching people to control
their appetites?" He changed the subject.

The Law does not make us sinners. The Law
tries to make us strong enough to resist the many
temptations to sin to which the human being is
subject daily. Whereas Christianity might say
that the effort is futile, that we can never become
strong enough to resist sin (including the sin of
taking pride in our moral strength, like the body
builder who can't stop admiring himself in the
mirror), Judaism would insist that we owe it to
God to have the moral seriousness at least to try.

The second gift of the Law is the reassuring
message that we and our moral choices are taken
seriously at the highest level. There are three
ways to handle our instinctual urges: we can
yield to them, as animals do. We can try to suppress them, with the result that we spend so much
time and effort thinking about them that we become obsessed with them (the dieter who spends

all day thinking about food; the person for whom resisting sexual temptation becomes a full-time preoccupation). Or (and you know I've saved the best for last) we can *sanctify* them. We can apply rules of permitted and forbidden to them in a way that no other living creature can, and we can then go on to enjoy them within those limits.

Let's go back to my hypothetical lunch with a friend. Watching me scan the menu, he may suspect me of thinking, "Oh, would I love to order the ham, but that mean old God won't let me." But in fact, what is probably going through my mind at the moment is "Isn't it incredible! Nearly five billion people on this planet, and God cares what I have for lunch!" And God cares how I earn and spend my money, and whom I sleep with, and what sort of language I use. (These are not descriptions of God's emotional state, about which we can have no information, but a way of conveying the critical ethical significance of the choices I make.) What better way is there to invest every one of my daily choices with divine significance?

There is nothing intrinsically wicked about eating pork or lobster, and there is nothing intrinsically moral about eating cheese or chicken instead. But what the Jewish way of life does by imposing rules on our eating, sleeping, and working habits is to take the most common and mundane activities and invest them with deeper meaning, turning every one of them into an occasion for obeying (or disobeying) God. If a gentile walks into a fast-food establishment and orders a cheeseburger, he is just having lunch. But if a Jew does the same thing, he is making a theological statement. He is declaring that he does not accept the rules of the Jewish dietary system as binding upon him. But heeded or violated, the rules lift the act of having lunch out of the ordinary and make it a religious matter. If you can do that to the process of eating, you have done something important.

We sanctify the act of eating with the dietary laws, the rules of keeping kosher. Because food is a highly emotional subject—it is more than just a matter of refueling our bodies; it is a symbol of love, of guilt, of reward, of weakness—there are lots of jokes about the Jewish dietary laws. (Catholic priest to his friend the rabbi: "You don't know what you're missing by not eating bacon. Why would God have created something so delicious if He didn't want people to enjoy it? When are you finally going to break down and try some?" Rabbi: "At your wedding, Father.")

There is also a lot of misunderstanding about the rules of keeping kosher. Many Jews and non-Jews alike assume the laws have to do with problems of keeping food from spoiling in desert conditions without refrigeration, or with obscure diseases one can get from eating pork. The problem is, first, you can get just as sick from eating bad chicken as from eating bad pork, and second, is it conceivable that no other people except the Israelites noticed that meat spoiled in hot weather? Do you really need religious rules to keep people from eating contaminated food?

The fact is that the rules of keeping kosher have nothing to do with trichinosis or contamination. They have everything to do with taking the process of eating, which we share with all other animals, and making it a uniquely human activity by investing it with considerations of permitted and forbidden.

For example, and very few of us know this, there is a Jewish law forbidding us to eat standing up. Animals eat standing up. Human beings turn the act of ingestion into a much more dignified one. They sit, they offer a prayer of thanks, they eat their food in a leisurely manner rather than gulp it as animals do.

The major Jewish dietary laws rest on a single premise: *Eating meat is a moral compromise.* There is a difference between eating a hamburger and eating a bowl of cereal. For one of them, a living creature had to be killed. Should we ever become so casual about the eating of meat that we lose sight of that distinction, a part of our humanity will have shriveled and died.

At times, the Torah would seem to imply that if people were morally perfect, they would be vegetarians. Adam and Eve are told to eat fruits and plants (Genesis 1:29), and giving Noah permission to kill and eat animals for food (Genesis 9:3) seems to be a concession to human weakness.

I was once invited to speak to a college audience, and the young woman in charge of the program asked me if they could arrange for the planning committee to have dinner with me before my lecture. I told her that would be fine, but I was a vegetarian, and would she please make the appropriate arrangements. She responded, "Oh, I wish I could be a vegetarian. I love animals and I hate the thought of killing them, but I also love chicken and steak and I don't think I could give them up. I feel so hypocritical about it." I told her that the Jewish dietary laws were meant precisely for people like her, as a way of permitting but restricting the eating of meat, letting you enjoy it within limits, and never letting you forget that you were free to enjoy it but it was a compromise. The prohibitions, the limitations would keep you from feeling guiltily self-indulgent about eating meat at all. Our family, which for many years ate kosher meat, has gradually become vegetarian for a combination of religious, moral, and health reasons. We see it as an extension of the discipline and sensitivity inculcated by keeping kosher. Some Jewish authorities, though, are suspicious of vegetarianism, for fear that it blurs the distinction between the value of a human life and that of an animal.

So we are permitted (at times even *commanded,* as with the Passover sacrifice of a lamb) to kill and eat animals, but that permission is hedged around with a series of limitations to ensure that we never do so casually.

1. Only certain species are permitted (cows, sheep, chicken, fish) and others (pigs, shellfish) forbidden. I am not sure there are reasons for including one and prohibiting another. People have tried to find ecological and hygienic reasons, but with limited success. It may be that the forbidden animals had personality traits from which people wanted to dissociate themselves; birds of prey are nonkosher, while gentler birds are permitted. Or it may simply be an arbitrary division, a way of introducing categories of permitted and forbidden to keep us conscious of what we are consuming.

2. When an animal is slaughtered, it must be slaughtered in as painless a manner as possible. This is why, when my non-Jewish friend and I go to lunch together, I must not only forgo the pork

and lobster on the menu, but I can't have the beef or chicken either, because presumably they have not been killed in a kosher manner. It may not make a whole lot of difference to the cow, which would prefer not to be slaughtered at all. But it should make a difference to us whether, in our compromise to kill for our dinner, we have taken care to minimize the animal's pain. That is why the Torah includes a law against slaughtering a calf in the presence of its mother. A Jewish ecology, defining our relationship to the earth and the creatures that inhabit it, would not be based on the assumption that we are no different from other living creatures. It would begin with the opposite idea: We have a special responsibility precisely because we *are* different, because we know what we are doing.

3. There can be no mixing of meat and dairy products at a meal. Once again, the reason has to do with holiness, not with health. We who buy our meat wrapped in cellophane and our milk in wax cartons have forgotten where those foods come from. Nature creates milk in the udders of mother animals to nourish their newborn young and keep them alive. To kill a young animal for meat is already a concession to human appetite. To combine that meat with the milk its mother produced to feed it is to compound the cruelty.

It was apparently the custom among the pagan

tribes who in biblical times were Israel's neighbors to take a baby lamb or kid and, as a special treat, instead of cooking it in boiling water, cook it in the milk with which its mother's udders were overflowing. This is why the Bible, shuddering at such gratuitous cruelty, phrases the basic prohibition "You shall not boil a kid in its mother's milk" (Exodus 23:19, repeated in 34:26 and twice more in Deuteronomy). Later sages, in their explication of the Oral Law (which will be discussed later in this chapter), decided that it would be just as insensitive on our part to cook the flesh of one animal in the milk of another, even if it were not its mother. As a result, observant Jews will not serve butter with a meal containing meat, or put cream in their coffee at such a meal. They will have separate sets of dishes and silverware for meat and dairy meals.

One more note: You may get the impression from what I have written that, for the traditional Jew, eating is hedged around with so many religious restrictions that there is not much left to enjoy. Not so; we Jews eat very well. Should you have the opportunity some weekend, try this anthropological experiment. Attend a non-Jewish wedding on a Saturday and a Jewish wedding on Sunday, and compare the attitudes toward food, the amount, the variety, and the gusto with which it is consumed. I suspect there is a simple psychological process at work, and it holds true for sexual behavior and other areas of human activity as well as for eating. Once you have marked the limits of permitted and forbidden, you can let yourself go and enjoy yourself within the limits of the permitted without wondering if you might be doing something wrong.

We sanctify our sexuality with rules about permitted and forbidden sexual contact. Along with hunger, the sexual drive is as strong a basic instinct as there is. After all, without it the species would not survive. It is another instinct we have in common with the animals. We had a dog, a female Welsh corgi, for fifteen years. When she would come into heat, male dogs for blocks around would leap over high fences and nearly break down our doors trying to get at her. Every now and then, there will be a story in the newspapers about some human adult driven equally mad by sexual desire, to the point where he squanders fortune and decency.

Some religions saw the sexual urge as divine because it was so powerful. (What, after all, are most books, most songs, and most movies about? Not food, money, or theology. They are about sexual attraction.) Others saw it as demonic, feared it, and made it the goal of the religious life to suppress it. Judaism, typically, set out not to make it disappear but to control it and thus to sanctify it, to make it yet another area in which to glorify God. As with food, we sought ways to enjoy it within limits, another instance of the Jewish belief that nothing God made was intrinsically good or evil. It all depends on what we do with it. Thus:

1. Jews are religiously obligated to marry and have children. There is no virtue in the celibate life. God has given us reproductive organs to be used. Some people, for reasons of temperament or ill fortune, will never marry. Others will marry and find themselves unable to have children. Judaism attaches no stigma to such people, but regards them as victims of circumstance, unable through no fault of their own to know one of the most fulfilling experiences of the human life. A blind man is not a sinner for never enjoying a sunset, and an infertile couple are not sinners for not having the experience of parenthood. But we must acknowledge that they are missing something.

2. Sexual activity is limited to married couples, and limited to certain times even within marriage. Adultery is wrong, not because the wife is the husband's property but because sexual contact is so uniquely intimate an activity (the husband actually entering inside the wife) that it belongs only in the framework of an ongoing

intimate relationship. Human beings are the only creatures who engage in sex face to face, because only to human beings does it matter with whom you are making love.

But even within a marriage (and this is something a lot of us don't know), Torah law forbids sexual intimacy while a woman is menstruating, and for several days afterward. I am not sure why. As with the dietary laws, the Torah sets forth the prohibition without giving reasons, although taboos and superstitions about menstruating women are widespread in many cultures.* It may simply be aesthetic discomfort with the menstrual flow. It may be the sense that menstrual blood is seen as containing some magic power, the secret of life, and a man must keep his distance from it. It may be, as one modern writer has suggested, a kind of mourning for the potential life that was not conceived that month. Or it may simply be a way of regulating sexual activity to

---

* English translators of the Bible are frustrated at trying to translate the traditional Hebrew term for a menstruating woman. They inaccurately render it as "unclean" or "impure." The Hebrew word has no such connotations of being dirty or bad. It more nearly has connotations of being touched by the holiness of the life force so strongly during those days, and also after giving birth, that a woman is unapproachable in normal ways.

maximize the possibility of procreation and childbirth. Which brings me to my third point.

3. Judaism sees sexual relations as a legitimate source of pleasure and not only as a means of making babies. That is why I feel entitled to perform wedding ceremonies for couples beyond the age of childbearing and for young women who have had hysterectomies. Parenthood is more than a consequence of following one's sexual urges. It is a religious obligation, a response to the command of God who began by creating life and told the first humans to be fruitful and multiply. But our tradition also recognizes the legitimacy of our need for intimacy, for feeling loved and cherished, and for loving and cherishing in return.

Judaism sanctifies the acquisitive instinct through tzedaka/*charity and through Sabbath rest.* There is a legend in the Talmud that one day people captured the Spirit of Selfishness and locked it in a closet. They rejoiced in their achievement, saying, "From now on, life on earth will be Paradise. There will be no selfishness, no cheating, no stealing, no competing to see who is better. We will have brought about heaven on earth." The next morning, no shopkeepers opened their stores. No young men went courting. No marriages were arranged. People did not bother to show up for work.

By noon, the people realized what they had done. Reluctantly, they let the Spirit of Selfishness out of its closet, and began to learn to live in a world where selfishness is sometimes the motivation for making good things happen.

As the legend suggests, to be acquisitive—to want the nicest house, the most attractive mate—is normal and human. As with food and sex, the world could not continue if we eradicated that impulse from the human soul. But to let that competitive, acquisitive instinct rule us so that we come to regard everyone around us as a potential customer or a potential rival, so that no matter how wealthy we are, we cannot stop hustling and cheating to acquire more, is to distort the image of God in which every one of us is fashioned.

Two major Jewish institutions serve as "calisthenics" to teach us to control our acquisitiveness without asking us to become so otherworldly that we forgo all the goods of this world in a kind of economic celibacy. One is the Sabbath, not only a day of rest from arduous physical labor, but a truce in the economic competition between us and the people around us. We will have more to say about the Sabbath in the next chapter, dealing with the Jewish calendar.

The second is the obligation of *tzedaka,* which is usually translated as "charity" but really means something closer to "doing the right thing." (Another example of the difficulty of trying to understand a culture while studying it in translation.) Charity implies that I give to the poor because I am a generous person. *Tzedaka* means that I give to the poor, even if I don't feel like giving, because Judaism tells me I should. It tells me that God has chosen to make me His intermediary in passing something on to the poor, so that I will be included in the good deed, but I have no right to keep that portion of my wealth for myself any more than the postman has the right to keep for himself a check addressed to me.

If you saw the play or movie *Fiddler on the Roof,* you may remember an exchange early in the play in which a man gives a beggar a coin. The beggar tells him, "Last week, you gave me more." The man answers, "I had a bad week," to which the beggar responds, "Just because *you* had a bad week, why should I suffer?" The exchange accurately captures the Jewish view that *tzedaka* is an obligation, not an act of charity.

I hesitate to make too much of this, but we may have a philosophical difference between Judaism and Christianity here. Is the purpose of charity to inculcate generosity in us or to provide sustenance for the poor? Both, obviously, but I think Christianity would emphasize the former a shade more, and Judaism the latter. In that famous passage in the Gospels (Matthew 26:6-13) in which a woman pours expensive oil on Jesus' head and the disciples scold her, saying she could have sold the oil and given the money to the poor, Jesus supports the woman, saying, "You will always have the poor with you"—that is, what you don't do for the poor today, you will be able to do for them tomorrow or next week—"but you will not always have me." The words "the poor you will always have with you" come from the Torah, in the Book of Deuteronomy, *but there they have the exact opposite meaning.* "For the poor shall never cease out of the land; therefore I command you to open your hand to your poor and needy brother." In other words, because there will always be poor people, society has to find a way of sustaining them without making them depend on your having some money left over after your shopping and vacation.

My friend Dennis Prager, a writer and Los Angeles radio personality, likes to present this problem to classes of young people: A man who is down on his luck tells his sad story to two passersby. One is moved to tears, embraces him, and gives him five dollars because that is all he can afford. The second man interrupts him halfway through and gives him fifty dollars just to shut him up. Who has done a better thing? The young people, all of whom have been raised to believe that feelings are more important than deeds, regularly choose the first person because his heart was in his gift. But Prager tells them that by Jewish law, the second man was better because fifty dollars will help the beggar ten times as much as five dollars will, and the purpose of *tzedaka* is to help the poor, not to give us opportunities to feel virtuous.

Now before you cry "Pharisaism!" and criticize the external gesture without any inner feeling (the Pharisees were the conspicuously pious Jews of the first century, and while most of them were sincere and some of them were saintly, enough of them were hypocrites to give them a bad name), let me point out an interesting psychological phenomenon. After a few occasions of giving charity for the wrong reasons (to feel potent, to impress the solicitor, to win God's favor, or to see your name on a plaque), something remarkable happens. You see how good it feels, and you start to give for more honorable reasons.

I remember when I was active in the civil rights movement in the 1960s. Some people urged us to delay passing laws for southern blacks to gain equal access to public facilities because society wasn't ready for it. But President Johnson and others correctly predicted, "Let them treat their black neighbors as equals not because they want to but only because the law requires it. Their hearts and minds will follow their behavior soon enough."

Whatever our philosophical position on the subject of good deeds with or without generous feelings, it remains an important teaching of Judaism that our money is not really ours, no matter how hard we may have worked for it. It is a gift from God, and God has instructed us to share a portion of it with the less fortunate.

In three generations, we American Jews, through education and hard work, have become a remarkably successful community, carving out a place for ourselves in the middle and upper-middle class of American society (though there is no shortage of poor Jews, many of them elderly). But we are a remarkably charitable community as well. We give generously to Israel and to Jewish causes and institutions in this country, and we give just as generously to the Red Cross, United Way, and medical research, to museums and symphonies. I know of several predominantly Jewish country clubs where one of the requirements of membership is that you document your having given a certain percentage of your annual income to charity. Prospective members may not enjoy that requirement at first, but they learn to like it.

We sanctify our power of speech. Food, sex, and a sense of territoriality are all things we share with other animal species. But we are challenged to sanctify the ordinary in one other area that is unique to us human beings, the gift of speech. While some would claim that "talk is cheap," in Judaism words are real. (The Hebrew language uses the same term, *davar,* to mean both "word" and "thing.") Children may chant, "Sticks and stones may break my bones but names will never hurt me," but even as they say that, they know it is not true. They know that their physical bruises will heal rapidly but they will remember taunts and insults for a much longer time. Jews take words seriously (is that why so many psychiatrists and so many of their clients are Jewish?) because, since the Temple was destroyed nineteen hundred years ago and we no longer bring animal offerings, words are the currency of our transactions with God. On Yom Kippur, we apologize for more sins of the tongue than for any other category of misdeed. So Judaism bids us use words to heal, to comfort the sick and the grieving, to bring peace between enemies. And it forbids us to use our divinely given power of speech, the same power that lets us communicate with God, to gossip or humiliate. The Talmud goes so far as to say that embarrassing a person and causing him to blush, or insulting him and causing him to turn pale, is a form of bloodshed.

Notice what has been the theme of every subject we have discussed in this chapter. If you can take the acts of eating, speaking, working, and making love, and invest them with religious significance, you have done a lot to liberate the religious impulse from the confines of the house of worship. It means, for one thing, that you don't have to find time in a busy schedule to be religious. You can be religious in the way you treat food, money, sex, not only the way you treat the Bible. You can be religious in the way you handle your checkbook, not only your prayer book, in the way you speak to your child or your neighbor as well as the way you speak to God. Do that and you will have done a lot to take the everyday and make it holy.

The unit of Jewish religious currency is the *mitzvah,* the literal translation of which is "commandment," as in the terms *Bar Mitzvah/Bat Mitzvah.* But functionally, a *mitzvah* is something you do because you recognize that you are supposed to do it as a Jew. Anything from lighting the Sabbath or Hanukkah candles to writing a check to protect the environment can be a *mitzvah* if you do it as a way of living out your Jewishness. When a traditional Jew performs a *mitzvah,* she prefaces it with a prayer: "Praised are You, 0 Lord our God, Ruler of the World, *who has brought holiness into our lives* by teaching us to perform the mitzvah of . . . [for example, lighting the Sabbath candles]." As my teacher Max Kadushin used to point out, to say "Praised are *You,* O Lord . . .', is to imply that God is present. We come into the presence of God, we reenact the moment of Sinai, not so much by going to a certain place, but by translating our Jewish identity into action wherever we are by performing a *mitzvah.* We bring holiness into our lives not by entering a sanctuary, but by acting to sanctify the everyday, making the ordinary extraordinary.

Where do all these rules come from? Some of them, but not all of them, are found in the Torah. Who invented the others? Jewish life is based not only on Scripture, but on what we call the Oral Law, a body of interpretation of the Torah by learned scribes and sages. Jewish life is based not just on the Bible, but on twenty-two centuries of interpreting the Bible.

For example, one of the Ten Commandments is "Thou shalt not steal." But what is stealing? If I take something from a friend without his permission because I am pretty sure he would let me have it if I asked him, is that stealing? If I find a lost object and keep it, though I suspect that with a little effort I could locate the owner, am I stealing? (By the way, the answer in both cases is yes, you are.)

Again, another of the Commandments tells us not to work on the Sabbath. But what is "work"?

Is it only what I get paid for doing? Is building a fire work? Is walking two miles uphill to the synagogue work? Is cooking my dinner work? (Answers: No, Yes, Maybe, Yes.)

Many of the rules of the Torah are not self-explanatory. They require interpretation. One of the most important developments in the history of Judaism occurred around the year 450 B.C. The king of Persia sent a man named Ezra to Jerusalem as his personal representative to shape things up in the Persian province of Judea. When Israel had been conquered by the Babylonians a century earlier, the Jews stopped existing as a political entity with a homeland of their own. The king of Persia wanted Ezra to reorganize them as a religious group in the Persian Empire, not a political one. Ezra established the Torah as the basic law by which all Jews would live. But he did something further. Acting on his reputation as the most learned man in the community, and brandishing his writ of authority from the king, he said that henceforth there would be no more revelation, no more prophets. God has said to us what He had to say. From now on, no one would be able to say, "Thus says the Lord. . . ." In place of revelation, there would be interpretation. We would become the People of the Book (though the phrase would not be coined until the time of Mohammed a thousand years later). If you need to know what God wants of you, don't consult an oracle or wait for a prophet to tell you. Read the Torah, and if the answer isn't clear, read it again more carefully or consult an expert.

The implications of this policy were of major significance. It meant that Jews had to be literate in a world where most people were not. It meant that the most important people in the Jewish community were not the strongest, the best-looking, or the richest, but the most learned, because only they could deduce accurately how God wanted us to live. As a result, an "aristocracy of intellectuals" developed, in which a person of humble origins, if he showed the ability to understand the classic texts, could become a prominent leader. A century or two ago, in the Jewish communities of Eastern Europe, it was common for the wealthiest man in town to approach the yeshiva, the Jewish academy, to arrange a marriage between his daughter and the brightest student.

The scholar Ernest van den Haag has a theory to explain the impressive intellectual achievements of Jews. He suggests that during the Middle Ages, the brightest young men in the Jewish community were encouraged to marry early, live a life of subsidized study, and have lots of children, while the brightest young men in Catholic society were encouraged to enter the priesthood and remain celibate. I am not sure he is right. I think the answer may be simpler: In a community that celebrates athletes, all the young men will want to be athletes, and the most talented ones will emerge. In a community that honors wealth, everybody will try to get rich, and the most able or the most ruthless will succeed. In a community that respects learning, everyone will try to excel at learning. (I once served as rabbi to an affluent Long Island congregation where millionaire industrialists would boast of the success and upward mobility of their children who were earning $30,000 a year as college teachers. They thought their children had surpassed them.)

Periodically, the Oral Law was written down, most prominently in the Talmud, so that it could be disseminated and studied. But while the written text of the Torah could not be changed, the Oral Law was always subject to expansion and revision. Obscure biblical precepts could be clarified. Outdated laws referring to an agricultural society could be updated to meet the needs of a commercial society. New laws could be drafted to deal with new problems (modern medical procedures, space travel), and with the transition from a world where non-Jews were hostile idol-worshippers to one where non-Jews were more likely to be friendly Christians sharing the same monotheistic heritage.

But all of these new laws had to be traced

back to the Bible. One could never say, "Since the Bible is silent on the subject of organ transplants, we are free to rule as we see fit." One had to say, "What biblical insights and teachings can guide us to taking a biblically correct position on organ transplants?"

An analogy would be to the attitude of the United States Supreme Court to the Constitution. Called on to rule on issues the Founding Fathers could never have contemplated, the court nevertheless has to base its decisions on principles enunciated in the Constitution because that is what gives its rulings legitimacy, even as the Torah does to the decisions of Jewish sages today.

For most of Jewish history, we lived by these laws. The divisions we know today among Orthodox, Conservative, and Reform Jews did not exist. You had no Orthodox Jews; you had observant Jews. The typical Jew did what Jewish law told him to do, not because he held certain theological positions but because he felt Jewish. Of course, there were Jews who gossiped, Jewish merchants who cheated their customers, Jews who slept late on wintry mornings and never made it to the synagogue. But for the most part, the remarkable thing is that the system set forth in the Book of Exodus worked. A community of ordinary people added up to something extraordinary. The whole was greater than the sum of its parts. Jewish communities in the Middle Ages (and in countries like Russia, the Middle Ages lasted into the twentieth century) were self-contained units, separated from their non-Jewish surroundings in everything except the most basic commercial contacts. They may have lacked wealth, fame, and intellectual brilliance, but they never lacked holiness. Everyone was literate, everyone was sober, husbands and wives were faithful to each other, not because they were afraid of God's judgment but because that was what people around them expected of them. Poor families with no talent for theological speculation would begin and end their meals, meager as they might be, with a prayer of thanks. People who could barely provide for their own needs would share what they had with widows and beggars, because they recognized the obligation of giving *tzedaka.* Sabbaths were observed and holidays were celebrated. God's strategy was successful—don't expect people to rise above their surroundings; fashion communities where sanctifying the ordinary moments of life is normal.

All that changed when the medieval world gave way to the modern and people began to think of themselves as individuals rather than as members of a recognized group. The modern world offered Jews the option of leaving the self-contained Jewish community and participating in the wider non-Jewish world as individuals whose Jewishness was not necessarily their most important trait. The first organized response to modernity was the Reform movement, which began in nineteenth-century Germany and flourished in Western Europe and the United States. Reform Judaism tried to locate Judaism's center of gravity in the ethical ideals of the Bible, which all of Western society had in common (and which had undeniable Jewish roots), and deemphasized the rituals that separated Jew from gentile. Religion, they claimed, should not be a barrier to our full participation in the best that society had to offer. It should stress what connected people more than what separated them. (To a great extent, Reform Judaism followed and justified the participation of Jews in modern society rather than causing it. It did not encourage observant Jews to become less observant. It addressed Jews who were leaving Judaism for the wider world, and told them, "You can do all that, and still be a good Jew.")

The response to the Reform movement became what we know as Orthodoxy. Orthodoxy is different from the life of observance that prevailed in Jewish communities in premodern times because it adds a layer of self-conscious theological/intellectual belief to the pattern of "doing what Jews do." It sees the process of change and adaptation as threatening the integrity of Judaism. Where the medieval Jew saw the performance of a *mitzvah,* a religious deed, as an opportunity to sanctify the daily moments of his life, the Orthodox Jew saw it as that, but also as a test of his loyalty. If there is a conflict between the will of God on the one hand and the convenience or customs of modern society on the other, which will win the heart of the contemporary Jew?

It should not surprise us that Reform Judaism flourished in Germany, France, and England, where "participating in the gentile world" meant the university, the opera, good food, and wine, while Orthodoxy prevailed in nineteenth-century rural Russia and Poland, where to the average Jew, "the gentile world" consisted of illiterate peasants who regularly got drunk and beat their wives. Why would anyone want to compromise his Jewishness to be part of that?

As the nineteenth century gave way to the twentieth and many European Jews crossed the ocean to the United States, a third alternative emerged, the Conservative movement. (Full disclosure: I was raised and educated in the Conservative movement, and served as a Conservative rabbi for my entire career. While I am trying to be fair, I cannot claim to be objective.) The premise of Conservative Judaism is that, just as a healthy human body is constantly sloughing off dead cells and growing new ones, so Judaism when it is healthy constantly sheds forms and customs that no longer serve their original purpose and creates new ones to meet changing conditions. This is what happened throughout Jewish history until modern times. Under the impact of modernity, Reform Judaism responded too rapidly and drastically to the rapidly, drastically changing conditions. It discarded elements of Judaism (Sabbath rituals, Hebrew prayers) that could have been retained and in fact would later be rediscovered and reintroduced. At the same time, Orthodoxy felt too threatened by the Reform movement to make even those necessary and permissible changes that might have come about in earlier, less defensive times.

All these movements have worked out ideological statements, theories about God, Revelation, and the Bible, to support their claims. But I have always suspected that the question of whether one chooses to be a Reform, Conservative, or Orthodox Jew depends less on what theory of Revelation you accept, and more on how much you want to participate in the life and lifestyle of the non-Jewish world around you. How much of that lifestyle are you prepared to sacrifice because you are loyal to Judaism? (I remember the Los Angeles Dodgers losing the 1966 World Series to Baltimore because Sandy

Koufax would not pitch the opening game, which fell on Yom Kippur.) The Reform movement flourished when American Jews felt strongly that they wanted to be like everybody else. In recent years, we have seen an unexpected resurgence of Orthodoxy, not because people's theology has changed but because American life, in all its vulgarity, has become less attractive to many sensitive young people.

So, for example, Reform Jews would feel free to eat anything in a restaurant (though many would avoid pork products). Orthodox Jews would eat only in a restaurant where all the food was kosher under strict rabbinic supervision. And Conservative Jews would avoid the meat and shellfish and eat salads, tuna sandwiches, or perhaps broiled fish.

Orthodox Jews would abstain from driving cars and using money or electricity on the Sabbath. Reform Jews would try to spend the day in appropriate spiritual/familial activities, some of which might be forbidden by traditional Jewish rules (watching television, driving to visit relatives, taking their children to an amusement park). And Conservative Jews would give themselves permission to drive their cars to the synagogue if it was too far to walk, and to turn on the radio or television to educational programs, concerts, or news, but not for programs that jarred the serenity of the Sabbath.

Orthodox services would be mostly in Hebrew and would assume that every congregant was knowledgeable enough to participate. Reform services would be overwhelmingly in English, with professionals doing most of the leading of worship and the congregation largely passive. Conservative services would be predominantly in Hebrew, with congregational participation in Hebrew singing and English readings, and some professional guidance for those unable to follow the service on their own. (I remember the reaction of one of my seminary professors, an Orthodox Jew, to the first Conservative service he ever attended. He was shocked by the custom of the rabbi announcing pages for the benefit of those worshippers who could not follow without help. He said, "It was like going to a dinner party and having the host announce, 'We will now all eat the salad with the small fork to your left.' ")

Two other trends in Judaism deserve mention. In the late eighteenth century, the Hasidic movement arose in Eastern Europe as an effort to bring a more emotional tone into the overintellectualized Judaism of that time, and to emphasize that God loved all Jews, even those who lacked the capacity for studying Talmud. Hasidic Jews today are even more insular and rejecting of the non-Jewish world than their Orthodox brethren. Where an Orthodox Jewish man can usually be recognized by his habit of wearing a yarmulka at all times, not only at prayer, many Hasidic Jews wear the distinctive garb of premodern Poland, where their movement arose, even on summer days in Brooklyn and Jerusalem.

And in the early twentieth century, my teacher Mordecai Kaplan shaped a movement known as Reconstructionism, which heavily influenced Reform and Conservative Judaism in the 1930s, '40s, and '50s. Where Reform Judaism taught that Judaism was essentially a set of religious affirmations and Orthodoxy saw it as being a set of prescribed deeds, Kaplan taught that Judaism was a community, a civilization. It embraced history, music, literature, language, and many things one does not ordinarily expect to find in a religion. It was Kaplan's thesis that the advent of the modern, individualistic world with its emphasis on personal choice called for a radical change (a "reconstructing") in what Judaism offered and asked of its adherents, as radical as the change called for by the destruction of the Temple in Jerusalem. If you think you see the influence of Mordecai Kaplan in the pages of this book and in my other writings, you are correct. (Dr. Kaplan died in 1983 at the age of one hundred two. As he approached his hundredth birthday, the joke among some of his students was that he would live forever because God, to punish him for his heresies, would never let him find out if there really was a heaven.)

Now that you have learned something about Reform, Conservative, and Orthodox Judaism, let me share with you the observation of a wise colleague of mine, that all of these labels and divisions are meaningless and obsolete. There are only two kinds of Jews, he says, serious Jews and non-serious Jews. Serious Jews try to do what Jews have always done, to bring holiness into their lives by sanctifying their everyday activities. They try to pattern their lives on the insights of Judaism, whether in a Reform, Conservative, or Orthodox idiom, while to the non–serious Jew, it doesn't matter what style of synagogue service he stays home from or which definition of *mitzvah* he ignores in his daily practice.

Many years ago, I attended a meeting of Christian and Jewish clergy, to which we all "brown-bagged" our lunches. The local Reform rabbi brought a ham and cheese sandwich, and before he began to eat it, he paused and recited the *motzi,* the traditional blessing over food. His Orthodox colleague said to him, "Aren't you being a hypocrite, saying that prayer over blatantly nonkosher food?" He replied, "Not at all. The Jewish dietary laws don't impress me as religiously valuable, but the habit of thanking

God for having food to eat impresses me very much." While I would differ with him on his evaluation of the dietary laws, I appreciate the seriousness of his response. The serious Jew will be recognized by his questions more than by his answers. The question "Who is a good Jew?" is not answered by checking someone's dietary habits or counting how often a person prays. A good Jew is someone who is constantly striving to become a better Jew.

This being the twentieth century, every reader of this book will be free to work out his or her own response to the web of Jewish observance. Where, for most of its history, Jewish observance was a set menu (in fact, the definitive guide to Jewish observance, written in the sixteenth century and still consulted by Orthodox Jews, is called *The Prepared Table,* that is, the set menu), today it has become a buffet where everyone gets to choose as much or as little as he wishes and doesn't have to put anything on his plate that he doesn't like. I have neither the right nor the power to tell you how to live out your Jewishness. I cannot tell you where to eat, when to pray, or how much to give to charity/*tzedaka.* I can only urge you to be serious. The question is not whether you will be Orthodox, Conservative, or Reform. It would be a shame if Reform Jews missed out on the sanctifying power of Jewish tradition because "we're Reform and we don't do those things." It would be equally sad if Orthodox Jews ended up going through the motions of rituals familiar to them from their childhood, without being awake to the remarkable sanctifying power of the things they do every day.

After a lecture I was giving one evening, I invited questions from the audience. One woman raised her hand, identifying herself as a Jew who tried to be a good and honest person, a helpful neighbor, and a supporter of Israel, but said that she did not live a religious Jewish life. She asked me, half seriously, half challenging, "Do you really believe that God will like me better if I kept kosher?" I told her that I was no authority on whether or why God liked some people better than others, but that was the wrong question. One didn't live a seriously Jewish life so that God would like you. Maybe that is what we were taught as children, but if so, that is only because children operate on that basis, not because God does. Children strive to do the right thing to win the approval of parents, teachers, and other important people in their lives (including, I suppose, God). If our perception of Judaism is still based on what we were told as children, we may well think in terms of doing things—going to services, keeping kosher, telling the truth—in order to please God.

But, I told her, if we can outgrow that childhood notion, we will come to understand that living a seriously Jewish life is not a matter of winning God's favor but of growing as a human being. Is God angry at you if you eat a cheeseburger? I can't believe He is. Do we disappoint God when we regularly reject the opportunity to turn breakfast, lunch, and dinner into religious moments, to raise them from the level of animal sustenance to the level of encounters with our humanity by imposing standards of permitted and forbidden on the foods we eat? Do we disappoint God and shortchange ourselves when we only worry about the food we eat nourishing our bodies, when we worry about its calorie count, cholesterol, and artificial ingredients, and never worry about choosing food so as to nourish our Jewish souls? That I can and do believe.

The question is not how many of the hundreds of *mitzvot* you choose to follow. The question is whether you are interested in doing what Jews have always done, recapturing the feeling of standing at Sinai, bringing holiness into your life by sanctifying even its ordinary moments, especially its ordinary moments. Over the centuries, ordinary people, people who were not saints, people who were not scholars, managed to do that, for God's sake and for the sake of their own souls. To paraphrase a familiar slogan, a soul is a terrible thing to waste.

4

Sanctuaries in Time: The Calendar

*H*OW DOES ONE keep alive that incredible feeling of encountering God at Sinai and feeling more human, more significant than you ever did before? One of the ways the Torah offers us is the setting aside of special days when ordinary concerns are transcended so that our souls are free to concentrate on the eternal, even as a married couple clears a day to mark their wedding anniversary, to recapture the way they felt about each other and what they promised each other on their wedding day, with a concentration their busy lives otherwise don't afford them.

Before we get to the specifics of the Jewish calendar and its red-letter days, let us consider for a moment what it means to have a second calendar to live by. We all throw out our old calendars on December 31 and begin a New Year on January 1. We all regulate our lives by the holiday breaks built into that calendar, looking forward to the Memorial Day weekend and the Fourth of July. But many of us regulate our lives by a second, parallel calendar. If we have school-age children, the new year begins in September and ends in June. Holidays and vacation times occur when the school says they do. If you are a professional baseball player (or a fan), the year begins in March and ends in October. If you are a retailer, the rhythm of your year is dictated by the holiday shopping season. There are factors regulating our sense of the passing of time and the change of seasons which our neighbors don't necessarily share. Having a second, parallel calendar can make life more interesting. It adds a second, private rhythm to your life as a counterpoint to the dominant rhythms of society. October may mean earlier sunsets to everyone, but will mean harvesting time to one family, foliage viewing to another, stocking winter merchandise to a third, and anticipating the World Series to a fourth.

As Jews, we share the general calendar with the rest of the population, running our lives by the public school calendar, the baseball schedule, and the demands of business just as everyone else does. But we have our own private Jewish calendar as well, and at times that helps keep us aware of things that others may not be thinking about.

You may have noticed that the major Jewish holidays fall at approximately the same season every year—the High Holy Days in the fall, Hanukkah in December near Christmas, Passover in the spring—but not always on the same date. The reason for that is that the Hebrew calendar is calibrated differently from the common one that we share with our neighbors. Our common calendar is based on the sun. A year is 365 days long, the time it takes the earth to make one full revolution around the sun. It is arranged so that the vernal equinox, the beginning of spring, with twelve hours of sunlight and twelve hours of darkness as the sun passes over the equator, will always fall on or around March 21, and the longest day, the first day of summer, will occur on or around June 21. The 365 days are divided into twelve months, usually thirty or thirty-one days long.

The Jewish calendar, with one interesting exception, is based on the moon rather than the sun. Each month begins with the appearance of the new moon, the first sliver of light after the moon has gone dark (the word *month* comes from the word *moon*) and lasts twenty-nine or thirty days, the time it takes for the moon to go through an entire cycle from new to half to full to half to dark again. Several of the important Jewish holidays occur on the fifteenth day of the month, when the moon is full. This has the double benefit of enabling one to keep track of the holiday's advent without a calendar, and scheduling the celebration at a time when the full moon provides natural night-time illumination. In our common, sun-based calendar, July 4 or December 25 or Election Day can occur anywhere in the moon's cycle.

(Trivia question: The last solar eclipse happened on the first day of the Jewish month. If a Jewish month averages 29½ days, what are the chances that the next solar eclipse will fall on the first day of a Jewish month? Trivia answer: A solar eclipse will always fall on the first day of a Jewish month. Solar eclipses happen when the moon comes between us and the sun, blocking out the sun's light. When that happens, the side of the moon that is turned to us is totally dark. That is a new moon, and the Jewish month would be beginning.)

The Jewish year consists of twelve months, alternating twenty-nine and thirty days in length, which add up to a year 354 days long, eleven days shorter than our common year. And this is where the interesting exception comes in, the only sun-based calculation in the Jewish calendar. If we simply let the calendar have its way, the Jewish year would be eleven days shorter than the common year, and every year the Jewish holidays would arrive eleven days earlier. Jews would have birthdays 3 percent more often than other people. This is what happens in the Moslem calendar, which is also moon-based. A holiday that comes in the spring this year will fall in the winter five or six years from now, and in the autumn several years after that. But that can't happen in the Jewish calendar, because Passover (for reasons we'll get to soon) has to come in the spring. So a very complicated and ingenious adjustment has been worked out. About every third year (seven times in a nineteen-year cycle, to be precise), to prevent Passover from coming before the vernal equinox (the first day of spring), a leap *month* is added in late winter, postponing Passover into the middle of April.

Two more technicalities: first, the Jewish day starts at sunset the previous evening, rather than at midnight. This is usually derived from the biblical expression used at Creation, "and there was evening and there was morning, the [first/second/third] day." But when you have grown up with the custom, it seems so logical for the weekday to yield to holiday while you are awake to welcome and celebrate it, rather than having it happen while you are asleep. And finally, I said earlier that the months of the Jewish calendar alternate between twenty-nine and thirty days, to coincide with the new moon, and that is basically true. But occasionally the length of the month is juggled by a day one way or the other, so that Yom Kippur, the Day of Atonement with its twenty-four-hour fast, never falls on a

Friday or Sunday where it would bump up against the Sabbath, and so that the seventh day of the Sukkot festival in the fall, when we pray for a year of abundance and economic prosperity, never falls on a Sabbath, when such prayers would be inappropriate.

Now to the specifics of the special days we are called on to celebrate.

The Sabbath

The holy days of the Jewish calendar have been called "cathedrals in time." For most of our history, we Jews have been a single people scattered over many geographical locations. Not since biblical times have most Jews been concentrated in the same country. Moreover, changing political fortunes and persistent antisemitism frequently forced us to migrate from a land we had lived in for generations and find ourselves a new home. Though we were always loyal and devoted citizens of the countries we lived in, we learned not to invest too much in the assumption that we would go on living there indefinitely. As a result, even when Jewish communities were prosperous, our synagogues were comfortable but modest structures. When you travel through England, France, and Germany, you marvel at the magnificent Christian cathedrals that brought people together to worship. There are no architectural masterpieces among the surviving synagogues of Europe. Instead, we created our cathedrals in time rather than space, in mood rather than stone. Instead of shaping granite, we learned to shape days into forms that would bring people together in reverence. The holiness of time was more portable and more democratically accessible than the holiness of space. When we wanted to feel ourselves in the presence of God, we did it not by going to a special place (even Jerusalem did not play this role in the Middle Ages, when travel was difficult and dangerous), but by giving the day a special shape and flavor. The best example of this is the Sabbath.

Along with our other major and minor contributions to world civilization, we Jews invented the weekend. Think about it: What does a week represent? A day represents the time it takes for the earth to rotate on its axis from sunrise to sunset to sunrise again. A month represents the cycle of the moon, from dark to full to dark. A year is the length of the earth's journey around the sun. But what is a week? A week is a human invention, an entirely manmade way of punctuating time. As such, it says something very profound about the freedom of human beings to control and dominate time.

Other animals are at the mercy of their biological clocks. Some of them are programmed to sleep by day and hunt at night, others are active in the daytime and sleep at night, but they have no choice in the matter. Human beings can turn on lights and schedule all sorts of activities when the world grows dark. Bears and other species hibernate during the winter rather than contend with the cold. We put on another sweater and keep on going to work. In most species, the female comes into heat at a certain season and males are driven to want to mate with her. Out of season, they are totally uninterested in sex. Human beings have the unique capacity to be sexually aroused at any time of the day, month, or year. We control time; time does not control us. And choosing to measure time in seven-day segments, as the Bible did for the first time in recorded history, is one of the ways we demonstrate that.

Another dimension of our uniquely human perspective on time is our sensitivity to differences between one day and another, indeed our ability to impose those differences. We decide to feel special on a certain day because it is our birthday or our wedding anniversary, and our deciding takes a day that is just like any other day everywhere except in our minds and makes it feel special. This is what Jews do with the Sabbath, running from sunset Friday to sunset Saturday.

We find two reasons in the Bible for making

the Sabbath special. The Torah takes the Sabbath so seriously that observing it is one of the Ten Commandments. (So much for the person who says, "I don't need prayers or rituals. Keeping the Ten Commandments is religion enough for me." There is an old Jewish joke about the rabbi who, during a sermon, points to the Ten Commandments and says, "You see, working on the Sabbath is exactly the same as committing adultery." At which point a congregant calls out, "I don't know about you, Rabbi, but I'm in a position to say they're not the same at all.")

The first reason the Sabbath is special is as a symbol and reminder of our having been freed from slavery in Egypt. Slaves have to work all the time; free men and women can take a day off for their own pursuits. In the ancient world, slavery was a question of who owned your body. Being able to sleep late and not put your body to the grind of hard labor was the sign of freedom. In the modern world, the issue of slavery is not a question of who owns your body, but of who owns your soul and who owns your time. The man or woman who suffers from the Thank-God-It's-Monday syndrome, who lives for his work and impatiently sees weekends as interruptions of what he really likes to do, is a slave. The highly paid executive who feels he can't take a vacation, who can't even take an afternoon off to watch his son pitch in a Little League game or go to his daughter's ballet recital, is a slave. He may own two homes, three cars, and an impressive stock portfolio, but if he doesn't own his own time, he is a slave.

Few of us completely own our own time. All of us have places where we have to be at a given hour to do a given job. But if at least once a week, we can claim a day for ourselves, we can feel free. I did my undergraduate work at Columbia University in New York City. I was surprised to learn that, at the time, Columbia owned Rockefeller Center, one of the most valuable pieces of property in midtown Manhattan. It had been given to the university by the developers, and leased back to the tenants, the income going for scholarships and other expenses. One day a year, Rockefeller Center was legally closed to traffic, as a symbolic statement to the world that Columbia owned it. That is what we do when we keep the Sabbath as a special day. We declare that, even if it seems on the other five or six days of the week that we belong to the various commercial interests we work for, we are in fact not slaves. We belong to no one but ourselves.

When, after the giving of the Ten Commandments at Sinai, the Book of Exodus begins to spell out how Jews should regulate their lives, the very first rule (Exodus 21:2) deals with granting slaves their freedom. If the Israelites should have learned one thing from their Egyptian experience, it is that God wants human beings to be free, to serve Him and not a human master. Claiming your right to rest on the Sabbath is a way of living out that idea. If you were taught about the Sabbath in Hebrew School as a set of prohibitions, telling you what you shouldn't be doing, you might want to start thinking about it instead as a right you are entitled to claim because you are a free person.

The second reason given in the Bible is a more subtle one: God created the world in six days and rested on the seventh. So we, too, are told to work for six days and rest on the seventh. (Another old Jewish joke: Tailor to customer: "Sorry, the pants aren't ready yet. Next week." Customer: "What's taking you so long? God made the whole world in just six days." Tailor: "I know, but look at the mess the world is in and look at how good the pants are coming out.") When we refuse to be beasts of burden, constantly working, when we insist on pausing to take stock of our work and to redefine ourselves by who we are and not just by what we do (why do we insist on answering the question "What do you do?" by describing how we earn our living?), we transcend the animal in us and let the godly dimension of our nature emerge. The two words used in biblical Hebrew to describe God resting on that first Sabbath are not the usual words for resting. The first means "He ceased His labors," and the second means "He got His soul back." We are commanded to rest on the seventh day first to demonstrate our freedom from slavery, and second to get our souls back.

We are commanded to rest on the seventh day, but "rest" is defined as more than sleeping late and doing nothing strenuous. It has at least three other dimensions.

First, Sabbath rest is defined as leaving the world alone, restraining our impulse to tinker with it. There will be six days coming up to work at fixing what is wrong with the world. For one day, let well enough alone. Sometimes the best way to solve a problem is to stop fussing with it and let it take care of itself.

Second, Sabbath rest is defined as freedom from obligation. You don't *have* to do anything. You don't even *have* to attend services; you are free to choose to attend, because you have a degree of leisure you don't have on other days. My own definition of Sabbath observance would involve taking my watch off at sunset Friday and not looking at it until sunset on Saturday, a luxury I could never afford when I was a congregational rabbi. There is perhaps no more oppressive, though necessary, taskmaster in our lives than the clock, as we rush to catch a certain train, fearful of being late, fidget nervously in traffic jams, interrupt what we are doing and enjoying because a favorite television show is coming on or we have to meet a schedule. A day on which I didn't know and didn't care what time it was would be a day of liberation for me.

And finally, Sabbath rest is a time of detaching ourselves for a day from all of our problems, everything unpleasant and unfinished. Even prayers for justice, health, and prosperity are eliminated from the Sabbath prayers, as we try not to dwell on the absence of justice, the lack of health in our lives. For one day, we try to see the world as it is supposed to be, free of pain and problems, to hold on to the vision of what it could be if we could just finally manage to get it right. We needn't worry; our problems won't disappear. They will all be there waiting for us at Sabbath's end—the unpaid bills, the family conflicts, the problems at work. But for one day, we will have had the liberating experience of not worrying about them. When the Torah commands us not to light a fire on the Sabbath, one commentator goes beyond the literal meaning of those words and takes them to refer to fires of anger and jealousy. Don't shout on the Sabbath, he advises us. Don't argue or get into fights. Don't raise your voice. That violates the Sabbath rest as much as actually starting a fire does.

Novelist Herman Wouk, who is an observant Jew, remembers the stressful days of preparing his play *The Caine Mutiny Court Martial* for its Broadway opening. Two weeks before opening night, when scenes were being rewritten and everyone was tense, Wouk went to the director on Friday afternoon and told him he was leaving and would be back again on Saturday night. "You can't do that," the director protested; "this is the most crucial period for a project in which people have invested hundreds of thousands of dollars." "I'm sorry," said Wouk, "but my religious commitments are more important to me than revising the play." As Wouk describes it, when he returned the following night, everyone else was still nervous, but he was mentally refreshed and able to see the problems in a new light and solve them.

I think the point of that story is valid; I know there are times the same thing has happened to me in my efforts to write. I would put my manuscript down on Friday afternoon even if I was at a crucial point, and after the Sabbath I was able to attack it with new energy. But one aspect of the story bothers me. One comes away from Wouk's testimonial with the sense that observing the Sabbath is worthwhile because it enhances your efficiency at work. Resting one day makes you a better worker on the other six. But I would like to think that Sabbath observance, like virtue, is its own reward, that it is worth doing not because it makes you a better worker, but because it makes you a better human being in those parts of your life that have nothing to do with work.

The ceremony of welcoming the Sabbath is one of the most magical moments of all of Judaism. When I speak to young couples about to be married about how to fill their home with Jewishness, when I talk to people searching for something to do differently to fill the spiritual vacuum in their souls, when young parents ask me how they can give their children more of a religious upbringing than they themselves had, the Friday night rituals of welcoming the Sabbath are the first thing I recommend. They work their magic even on people who are ordinarily not given to religious ritual. (By the way, the other things I recommend for the person who is taking his or her first steps in living more Jewishly are forming the habit of giving *tzedaka* and cleansing your speech of obscenities and malicious gossip. Try it; you'll be surprised how quickly you will start to feel like a different, nicer person.)

Do you remember the high school physics problem about the tree that falls in the forest with no one around to hear it; does it make a sound? In the same way, if the sun sets on a Friday evening and no Jew lit candles or sat down to a Sabbath dinner, would it still be *Shabbat* or would it just be Friday night? If we do nothing to make it special, Friday night is no different from Wednesday or Thursday night. We have the power and the responsibility to make it special, to sanctify it. Like so much else in Judaism, the Sabbath eve rituals testify to the power we share with God, the power to take the ordinary and make it special.

On Friday evening, the table is set more formally than on an ordinary weekday. The family will have arranged to eat together. No one drifts in late; no one runs off early. (A psychologist friend of mine tells me, to my astonishment, that the most reliable indicator of how well a student will do in high school is how often he eats dinner with his parents!) In a home where the wife and mother is present, she lights the candles and offers a blessing praising God for teaching her how to bring holiness into her home by performing the *mitzvah* of lighting Sabbath candles. There is also the lovely custom of her reciting a silent personal prayer for the well-being of her family: may all the coming week be as peaceful for all of us as this moment is. Where a wife and/or mother is not present, anyone can light the candles.

The lighting of the candles was originally a functional necessity rather than a religious ritual. In homes where there was no electricity, since you could not kindle a fire on the Sabbath, you would light candles at the last moment before sunset to help you see your way around the house. But the candles have come to symbolize much more—the presence of God in your home, symbolized as He so often is by a flame; the promise of warmth and light winning out over the cold and darkness outside. Traditionally, the candles are lit just before sunset. In summer, when the sun sets late, we light our Sabbath candles as we sit down to dinner, welcoming the Sabbath a few hours early. In winter, when the sun sets while family members may still be on their way home from school or work, the first one home may light the candles, but should wait until the family has gathered for the Sabbath meal to say the blessings over them.

In families where there are young children and the father is present, after the candles have been lit, the father blesses the children. He places his hands on their heads and recites the benediction "May the Lord bless you and keep you. May He send His light into your lives and deal graciously with you. May He look favorably upon you and grant you *shalom,* peace."

When our children were young, this was my favorite moment of the week. There is something deeply stirring about a parent blessing a child, telling them that he loves them and wishes them well. (How many adults are emotionally wounded today because they never heard their parents tell them they loved them?) This ritual has the virtue of telling you when and how to do it, instead of asking you to find the occasion and make up the words yourself.

The meal begins with *kiddush,* the prayer recited over the cup of wine, proclaiming the holiness, the specialness of the Sabbath, and the *motzi,* the prayer of thanks for the bread, and by extension all the food we are about to enjoy. The prayer over the wine cup says some interesting things about the Jewish attitude toward food, toward alcohol, and toward life. Religious traditions as diverse as those of the Southern Baptists and the Muslims forbid their followers to drink wine or any alcoholic beverage at all. They recognize its power, like the power of sex and greed, to make people do things they would ordinarily not do. But Judaism is consistent in its position that nothing God created is intrinsically sinful. We don't have to worship it or repress it; we can sanctify it. So wine—at a Sabbath meal or Passover Seder, at a wedding ceremony, or at the circumcision feast of a baby boy—symbolizes the idea that something special, something simultaneously joyous and sacred, is happening. (There is a theory that few Jews are alcoholics because we are taught from the beginning to associate wine with holiness rather than with self-indulgence.)

You may be attracted by the Friday night rituals of welcoming the Sabbath, by its promise of serenity and family sharing as a counterpoint to the frantic individualism of the other days of the week. But you may be put off by two considerations: Won't I feel self-conscious performing these rituals that I'm not accustomed to? And won't I feel like a hypocrite, suddenly doing these Jewish things I've never done before, when there are so many other Jewish things I don't do?

The answer to the first question is yes, you will probably feel awkward, uncomfortable, and self-conscious the first few times you light the Sabbath candles and say a prayer, just as you felt awkward and self-conscious in your first aerobics class, first tennis lesson, or the first time you tried a new recipe. But as in all those cases, the self-consciousness disappears after a few tries.

Are you being hypocritical if you suddenly start observing some Jewish rituals while omitting others? Not at all. A hypocrite is a person who publicly claims one set of values while privately living by another set. You would be a hypocrite if you claimed to be Orthodox while not practicing it, or claimed to be secular while keeping religious rituals when no one was watching. But I suspect that the real question behind the question is: Do I have to do everything to be a serious Jew, or can I do some things and not others?

The answer is that hardly anyone does everything, and we all pick and choose. Even the Orthodox Jew *chooses* to be observant. Some rare individuals go through a religious experience that moves them to reject their previous lifestyle and change everything at once. Most of us will find that neither necessary nor possible. If we are to grow in our Jewishness, we will do it by climbing the ladder of observance one step at a time. Welcoming the Sabbath is a good place to start. When you have mastered it and are ready for more, you can extend the sanctity of the Sabbath eve to the following day as well.

This is the paradox of the Sabbath: There is nothing holy about the day itself unless we pause to sanctify it. But when we do, we who are lacking holiness in our own lives find that the Sabbath somehow reflects holiness back into our lives and homes. I find it miraculous that, to a world burdened by the modern plagues of the tyranny of the clock and the office and by the decline of the family bond, this four-thousand-year-old institution offers the best cure.

The High Holy Days: Rosh HaShanah

The Jewish calendar year begins in the fall with a ten-day period of examining how we lived during the year that has ended, and articulating our hopes and prayers for the year ahead. What makes these days special is not only the profundity and solemnity of the prayers offered, but the fact that we take them so seriously. In the congregation I served for twenty-four years, the 270 seats in the sanctuary were usually more than adequate to accommodate the worshippers on Sabbaths and holidays. But for the High Holy Days every fall, we would open up the collapsible wall separating the sanctuary from the large multipurpose room behind it, set out an additional seven hundred seats, and then set up a tent in the parking lot for an additional four hundred worshippers. (And at peak moments of the service, we would still have people standing in the back and aisles.) Every year for twenty-four years, I would try to conduct a service so meaningful, and deliver a sermon so eloquent, that people would be moved to attend in similar numbers every week. And every year, the crowds would disappear after Yom Kippur and not be seen again till the following September.

I have never understood why we respond to the High Holy Days the way we do. In part, I think, the season catches our apprehension about what might happen in the year ahead. When we are young, we can hardly wait for our next birthday. We are eager to be a year older, to rush into the next chapter of our lives. But as summer yields to autumn in our personal calendars, our mood changes. We become less eager, more apprehensive. We are all too aware of the uncertainties of life, all too aware of the bad things that might happen to us and to those around us in the course of a year. We find comfort in community, in the presence of so many others around us sharing the same hopes and fears. And we find comfort in the liturgy's helping us articulate our hopes and fears in words more eloquent than we could have come up with ourselves.

The first two days of the holiday season are marked as Rosh HaShanah, the beginning of the year. The service is long, stately, majestic. Two themes dominate the Rosh HaShanah prayers. The first is the recognition of God as King. We sound the *shofar,* the ram's horn, as was done in ancient days to herald the arrival of the king. We chant psalms and prayers celebrating God's sovereignty over the world. Now, for much of human history, the metaphor of God as King was undoubtedly a very effective one. Ancient people probably had only the vaguest notion of who God was, but they understood who the king was. He was an all-powerful, awe-inspiring figure who made the laws and had power of life and death over his subjects. One trembled in his presence and strove to remain on his good side. (Even today, when the notion of kingship is more quaint than awesome, wealthy and sophisticated Britons and Americans get all excited at the prospect of meeting a member of the royal family. I recall a crowd gathering outside a London shop on the strength of a rumor that a royal visitor would be patronizing it.)

But for most of us, the metaphor of king no longer works. (Or perhaps it works too well. Many of us are likely to think of God as we think of, say, the king of Norway, a remote but genial chap, paid perfunctory honor and trotted out for holidays and ceremonial occasions.) What can the idea of God's sovereignty mean to us today? It can mean that someone is in charge of the world, that the world is not given over to chaos and anarchy but that there is order and purpose to it. (Jewish tradition has it that the world was created on Rosh HaShanah, though obviously that is a piece of information no one is in a position to know.) It can mean further that we are not the ones in charge of the world, that no matter how free and powerful we may be, individually or collectively, the world is not ours to control, exploit, or dominate. As the New Year begins, we are reminded of what our place in the world is—important and capable figures, but very much God's subjects.

The second theme of the Jewish New Year is the theme of the Day of Judgment. At the emotional climax of the service (and it is a very long and full service, the words and music combining for an effect of great solemnity), we invoke the metaphor of God sitting in judgment over all humanity, opening the books, scrutinizing the records of the past year, and passing sentence on each of us. "It is decided on Rosh HaShanah and confirmed on Yom Kippur, who shall live and who shall die, who shall prosper and who shall suffer, who shall be at ease and who condemned to wander. . . ."

My parents, who were both born in Europe, would describe how, at this point of the service, the women (who were seated in a separate section of a small, traditional synagogue) would begin to weep aloud as they contemplated all the possible disasters of the coming year. The men would begin to pray with increased fervor, a tone of anguish and pleading entering their prayers. As they chanted, "Who shall live and who shall die, who by fire and who by earthquake . . . ," they looked around them at their friends and neighbors, and wondered which of them (or perhaps they themselves) would no longer be there when the next New Year arrived.

My book *Who Needs God* was published just before the High Holy Days in 1989. Right after Yom Kippur, my publisher sent me to the West Coast for radio and television appearances to talk about the book. And so it happened that I was standing in front of a restaurant in downtown San Francisco on a Tuesday afternoon when the earthquake struck. It lasted only a few seconds, and minutes later I was one of a crowd of dazed, bewildered, but unharmed people crowding the downtown streets. As I walked back to my hotel, looking at cracks in the sides of buildings and hearing the sounds of fire engines, I found myself remembering the words of the High Holy Day prayer I had recited with my congregation just a few days earlier: "It is decided on Rosh HaShanah and confirmed on Yom Kippur who shall live and who shall die, . . . who by fire and who by earthquake. . . ." Could I believe, could I accept the notion that God had favored my prayer the previous week and decided that I would survive the earthquake while He condemned other people to die in it? I have seen too many good people die at the wrong time in the wrong way to believe that.

Maybe some Jews literally believe that God decides their fate for the coming year every September, with the sense of being freed from responsibility that such fatalism brings ("Why bother to buckle my seat belt or cut down on my smoking? When your number's up, it's up.") But I would hope that most of us realize the worst thing you can do to a poetic metaphor is to take it literally. We don't have to dismiss a tender and moving love poem because it contains a reference to Cupid's arrow and we no longer believe that love is caused by a cherub's shooting an arrow into our heart. And we need not either dismiss or accept literally the poetic metaphor of God sitting in judgment over us.

What can that image mean if we don't take it literally? It can mean that our deeds count, that God takes note of our day-to-day behavior and our ethical choices. (Our fate is based on an examination of our record.) It can mean that what kind of person we are matters to God. It can mean that we are ultimately held accountable for how we use the opportunities with which being alive and human presents us. Or it can mean that we are called on to turn to our faith to arm us against the uncertainties of the coming year.

The Torah readings on the two mornings of Rosh HaShanah tell the story of Abraham and Sarah, of their longing to have a child to carry on their family traditions, of the birth of Isaac when his parents were old, and of God's bizarre command to Abraham to take his son Isaac and offer him as a sacrifice. I have always believed that those readings were chosen to make the point that human history is the story of what happens to husbands and wives, to parents and children, and not what happens to kings and armies. When the entire congregation gathers for worship on Rosh HaShanah, the message they hear stresses the importance of passing on a tradition from generation to generation, from parent to child.

The story of the near-sacrifice of Isaac has always bothered me, as I suspect it has bothered many readers of the Bible. Why would God test the faith of His obedient servant Abraham by asking him to sacrifice his only son, and then intervene to stop it at the last moment? During the years that our son was alive but seriously ill and we never knew if he would survive the coming year, I found it a painful story to read. My interpretation now is that the story was originally an account of Isaac's going through an ordeal to mark his passage from childhood to manhood, and was later recast as a story of God's testing Abraham's faith.

After the Torah reading, the *shofar* is sounded, a series of shrill notes on a hollowed-out ram's horn. It has been interpreted as a dramatic way of proclaiming the presence of the King, as a kind of "wake-up call" to impress us with the urgency of the day, and as one of those experiences that are memorable because they transcend logic and have a mystical quality to them.

The last section of the Rosh HaShanah prayers consists of three series of biblical verses on the themes of Sovereignty (God is Lord of the Present, Ruler of the world), Remembrance (God is Lord of the Past; no good or bad deed is forgotten; everything we do matters), and Deliverance

(God is Lord of the Future, and will one day redeem His people and His world).

We come away from the long, majestic Rosh HaShanah service on the first days of the New Year with the message that living in God's world is a serious business and we have to rethink our priorities if we are to use rightly the New Year we have been given.

The traditional greeting on Rosh HaShanah is *L'shanah tovah tikatevu*—"May you be inscribed [in God's book] for a good year." On January 1, we wish each other a "Happy New Year" because the goal of secular society is to be happy. But on Rosh HaShanah, we remind ourselves that our real goal is not to strive for happiness, but to strive for goodness. If we do that, happiness will follow.

Yom Kippur

I know of no holiday in any other religion quite like Yom Kippur, the Day of Atonement. Other religions have days of fasting. Moslems abstain from food every day for a month during Ramadan, but only during daylight hours, feasting and celebrating after dark. Lenten "fasting" in those Christian traditions that still emphasize it means eating smaller meals with greater restrictions. But Yom Kippur is a twenty-four-hour period of total abstention from all food and water. The evening and the entire following day till sundown are spent in the synagogue in prayer.

Why do we fast on Yom Kippur? Not to punish ourselves as a way of making up for the weakness and self-indulgence of the past year (we would have to fast for much longer than one day to do that), and not to cause God to pity us when He sees how much we are suffering for His sake. We fast to prove, to ourselves as much as to anyone else, that we are human.

As we mentioned earlier, all other living creatures are "programmed" by instinct. Only human beings can say no to instinct. You can train a dog not to eat through fear of punishment, but you can never teach a dog voluntarily to go on a diet or to pass up food for ideological reasons. Only human beings can do that.

The King James translation of the Bible renders the command to fast on Yom Kippur as "ye shall afflict your souls," a kind of self-punishment, a flagellation. But more recent translations capture the original intent of the somewhat ambiguous Hebrew by taking the words to mean "you shall restrain your instincts, you shall practice self-control." Since religion is the effort to make people into human beings, and since Yom Kippur is the most "religious" day of the year in the sense that it is totally free of worldly distractions, we fast to show that we are capable of that supremely and uniquely human gesture, saying no to a basic instinct. Married couples refrain from sex on Yom Kippur not because sex is sinful or self-indulgent (any more than food is), but because a day of abstinence represents another symbol of control over a basic instinct.

One of the scriptural readings for Yom Kippur is taken from the second half of the Book of Isaiah, chapter 58. The people complain to the prophet that they have fasted and afflicted themselves, but despite their suffering, God has not answered their prayers. The prophet answers that the purpose of fasting is not to win God's sympathy but to help us develop a sense of empathy with the poor and the oppressed, with people who go hungry not out of choice or religious observance but out of necessity.

> Is such a fast I desire,
> A day for men to starve their bodies? . . .
> No, this is the fast I desire: to unlock the fetters
>   of wickedness,
> And untie the cords of the yoke,
> To let the oppressed go free, and share your
>   bread with the hungry. [Isaiah 58:5-6]

What do we do with the Day of Atonement after we have cleared it of all worldly distractions and freed it to be a day of examining our relationship to God? We use it to seek atonement and reconciliation, to ask God to forgive our failures and accept us as we are. During the year, we expend so much energy trying to be perfect, trying to convince others that we are perfect, that the mistake was their fault and not ours, that the business failure should be blamed on somebody else. As the bumper sticker puts it, "The man who can smile when things are going wrong has just thought of someone to blame it on." Nothing that goes wrong is ever our fault. We never seem to notice how much energy gets diverted into justifying ourselves at someone else's expense, or how our insistence that we are always right alienates us from the people around us.

But on Yom Kippur, we hear the liberating message "You don't have to try to fool Me by pretending to be perfect. I made you and I know better than anyone how weak and distractable you are. So don't try to impress Me by pretending to be someone you're not. Impress Me by trying to learn from your mistakes and be a little better than you've been till now. After all, I know who you are and I love you anyway." That word *anyway* (implied though not used literally in the Yom Kippur liturgy) is a powerfully liberating concept. It frees us of the necessity to justify ourselves, to insist that we are always right. It permits us to face up to our flaws, as the first step in doing something about them, without having to fear that we will be condemned or rejected for not being perfect.

Yom Kippur begins at sunset as the ninth day of the New Year fades into the tenth with the prayer *Kol Nidre* (All Vows). It is not so much a prayer as a legal formula, asking that we be released from all vows and promises we made last year and were not able to live up to, so that they not be held against us in the New Year. The reference is not to commitments we have made to other people, but vows and pledges to God to change and improve, promises we meant when we made them and feel guilty for not having kept. But as so often happens in Jewish liturgy, it is not the words but the music that makes the prayer so memorable. Especially because most of the prayers are in Hebrew, it is the music that communicates the mood of the service—joyous on the Sabbath, solemn and apprehensive on the High Holy Days, even when the words we recite are the same words. The music of Yom Kippur conveys a mood of human frailty and fallibility. We want to be more than we are, better than we are, but there seems to be a law of gravity that keeps pulling us down. Yet we never despair of trying to grow and to improve.

The effect of the Yom Kippur service is cumulative. We repeat the prayers hour after hour until our resistance to taking them personally is worn down. We confess that "we have cheated, we have spread malicious gossip, we have been self-indulgent in our eating and drinking, we have failed to honor parents and teacher . . ."— always in the plural, because as Jews, we come before God as a congregation, sustained by the merits of other Jews and implicated in their failures. But even as we recite the words "*we* have sinned . . . ," our thoughts are on where each of us has fallen short of what he or she might have been and how we can change.

Yom Kippur ends twenty-four hours after it begins with a service known as Neilah, "the closing of the gate." The image comes from ancient times when the gates to a walled city would be closed at sunset. As the day waned, you had to hurry to make it back before the gate closed and shut you out. Yom Kippur is an opening, a "window of opportunity" to look at ourselves without pretense and find ways in which we would like to be different to make the next Yom Kippur confrontation with Judaism's standards a less embarrassing one. If Yom Kippur, with its solemn power, with its cumulative force of hour after hour of prayer recited by the entire community together, cannot move us to change, whatever will? The gate will close and we will have missed the opportunity.

The Pilgrim Festivals

There is no connection between the three histori-cal-agricultural holidays known as the "pilgrim festivals"—Sukkot, Pesach or Passover, and Shavuot—and the Pilgrims who settled New England almost four hundred years ago (although there is a historical relationship between the Pilgrims and the Sukkot holiday). The word *pilgrim* is a corruption of the word *peregrin* and means "a traveler." Three times a year, on a specific date in the spring, summer, and fall, every Jew was to make a pilgrimage to the Temple in Jerusalem, to thank God for the harvest of food and to pray for more, and to thank God for His providential involvement in Jewish history as it once manifested itself at these seasons of the year.

What continually impresses me about the pilgrim festivals is how they succeed in combining the agricultural and historical dimensions of each season, blending past and present, nature and history. Think of it this way. There are two ways of looking at time. We can see time as cyclical, the same thing happening over and over. The hands of the clock trace their way around a circle over and over again. Tuesday follows Monday, and Wednesday comes after Tuesday week after week. Spring gives way to summer, which is followed by autumn and then winter. As Ecclesiastes puts it in the Bible, "The sun rises and then it sets and returns to the place of its rising . . . and there is nothing new under the sun."

Or we can see time as directional, not going around in circles but leading from somewhere to somewhere else. Every day is a brand-new day, one that has never existed before. Today is not just another Tuesday; it is a brand-new Tuesday. This month is not just another step in the recurrent cycle of the seasons. It is a blank new page in the calendar waiting to be filled in. The cyclical view of time is the domain of Nature; the directional view is the world of History.

The genius of the pilgrim festivals, as we will see when we examine them in turn, is their success in combining the two views of time, the worlds of Nature and History.

Sukkot / Tabernacles

Two things about the harvest festival of Sukkot will surprise you. First, you have probably been celebrating it annually all your life. And second, in ancient Israel this, not Yom Kippur, was the High Holy Day.

People living in the United States have celebrated Sukkot every autumn even if they have never set foot in a synagogue, because it was the prototype for the Pilgrim Thanksgiving. The Pilgrims were well acquainted with Scripture and knew that it behooved a man to give thanks to the

Lord for the bounty of the harvest. Gratitude is perhaps the fundamental religious emotion. Many people who are uncomfortable with religious rituals and scheduled worship services are capable of feeling grateful when things beyond their control turn out the way they hoped they would. This has been especially true for farmers, who understand that, no matter how hard they have worked, a successful harvest depends on forces beyond their control.

That instinctive feeling of gratitude was one of the two reasons for the Israelites thronging the Temple in Jerusalem on Sukkot. The other was the opportunity to pray to God for a good and bountiful harvest in the upcoming year, to invoke His blessing of abundant rain with prayers and rituals.

But if Sukkot had been only that, it would have been indistinguishable from the fall harvest festivals in many other agricultural societies. What made it unique was the Torah's grafting a historical theme onto the agricultural one. The little huts Jews lived in during the week-long holiday not only represented the tents farmers would sleep in at harvest time to be able to spend as many hours as possible in the field. (The Hebrew word *Sukkot,* often translated by the grandiose term *tabernacles*, really means "little huts.") They came to symbolize the temporary shelters the Israelites lived in during their forty years of wandering from Egypt to the Promised Land. The double theme of the holiday thus became: Lord, You were gracious to our ancestors during their years of wandering, leading them safely through the wilderness and bringing them to the Promised Land [History]. And You are gracious to us, their children, by causing the rain to fall and the food to grow [Nature].

We observe Sukkot today by building little shelters of our own—just a couple of temporary walls, some branches over them to form a partial roof, and fruit and flower decorations; think of it as the Jewish equivalent of putting up a Christmas tree—and enjoying food and wine in them at what is in much of the United States the nicest time of the year to be outdoors, the early autumn. Our synagogue prayers are accompanied by the ritual of taking in hand four plants that grow in the land of Israel. Their technical names are the *lulav* (palm branch with willow and myrtle leaves attached) and *etrog* (a kind of lemon, but not exactly). We may no longer be farmers whose calendar is timed to the rhythms of the harvest, but if we spend most of our time indoors in a world of electric light and artificial climate control, we will surely benefit from this reacquaintance with the outdoors.

The historical remembrance symbolized by

the *sukkah* shelters gave the agricultural holiday of Sukkot the additional dimension of expressing gratitude for having a roof over one's head, however modest. It became traditional for new homes to be dedicated and moved into at the Sukkot season.

For some, Sukkot's message is not only about gratitude for the past and hopes for future prosperity. It is about the impermanence of the things of this world. Our homes, like the frail *sukkah,* are vulnerable; the harvest will spoil if not gathered promptly. The beauty of autumn will give way to the barrenness of winter. Perhaps that is why the sages decreed the reading of Ecclesiastes, with its world-weary perception that "all is vanity," with its urging that we seize the moment and enjoy it before it passes, in the synagogue at the Sukkot season.

The last day of Sukkot week is a separate holiday, *Simchat Torah,* the day of rejoicing in the Torah. On that day, we complete the annual cycle of reading the Torah publicly, reading the closing lines of Deuteronomy, the death of Moses, and turning immediately to the opening verses of Genesis, the story of Creation, starting the whole annual process over again. Congregants carry the Torah scrolls around the synagogue, dancing with them as they go. I have always been impressed by the symbolism, as if we were saying that sometimes the Torah can be a burden (those scrolls can be heavy), but it is a burden we bear proudly and gladly. In the last years of the Soviet Union, *Simchat Torah* was the "High Holy Day" of Russian Jewry, the day on which they gathered outside Moscow's synagogue, singing and dancing, as if to say, "We proudly accept the burdens and disadvantages of being Jews in the Soviet Union. Despite all the government does to add to that burden, we would not give it up even if we could."

Pesach/Passover

I once heard Bishop James Pike define a Christian as a person who took the story of the Crucifixion and Resurrection personally. He then went on to define a Jew as a person who took the story of the Exodus from Egypt personally. In a real sense, Passover is where Judaism begins. This is what turned the descendants of Abraham, Isaac, and Jacob into a people summoned by God, a people into whose collective life God suddenly erupted with His liberating message.

The story recounted in the Book of Exodus is familiar. The Hebrew people were slaves in Egypt. They cried out to God, who visited a series of calamities on the Egyptians. Then God instructed the Israelites to sacrifice a lamb, to join in eating it together, and to mark the doorposts of their homes with its blood so that the last and most terrible plague would *pass over* their homes as it struck the homes of the Egyptians. In the aftermath of that last plague, Pharaoh finally relented and, at midnight under a full moon, let the Israelites go free. Because of their abrupt departure, they had no time to bake bread, so they quickly mixed some flour and water, baked a flat bread known as *matzo,* and followed Moses into freedom. As a perpetual reminder of that, we gather on the night of the first full moon of spring for a formal, ritualized meal (known as a Seder), at which no bread but matzo is eaten.

Scholars identify two strands of ancient holidays in the Passover observance. Shepherds would sacrifice a lamb in the springtime to give thanks to God for the new lambs that had just been born. (Nature in its wisdom arranges for lambs to be born in the spring when the climate is no threat to their survival.) At the same time, farmers would make an offering of the new wheat, which had just begun to ripen, as a similar gesture of gratitude. As winter ebbed, the typical family would be down to its last rations of wheat from the previous year's harvest. By March, the grain would not only be meager, it would probably be stale. When the new wheat was ripe, the family would, with a profound sense of relief and gratitude, clear out the old and celebrate the fresh grain. I was once driving through Idaho on vacation and heard a radio program advising farmers to discard last year's wheat before storing the new crop because the old grain was likely to be infested with vermin and would contaminate the new. This practice of discarding the stale, old grain is the origin of the custom of not only abstaining from bread, but getting rid of all fermented grain products for the week of Passover. In traditional homes, special dishes, never used for grain products during the year, are brought out for the week of Passover, and no foods containing even a trace of leavened grain—no cereal, no whiskey, no ice cream cones—are permitted.

But look at what our tradition has done to those springtime wheat and lamb festivals. It has added a moral-historical dimension. Just as spring is the time when new lambs are born, so it is the season when the Jewish people was born— out of the confinement of Egypt, through the waters of the Red Sea in a birth metaphor, into life and freedom. Just as spring represents the world's returning to life, liberated from the cold, barren months of winter, so it represents the liberation and the coming to life of an entire people. The lamb, the matzo are no longer only symbols of a farmer's gratitude. They carry the profound message that freedom is hard and expensive, that it asks you to give up a measure of your substance and your comfort on the road to independence.*

The Seder meal with which Passover begins shows the Jewish educational approach at its best. Special foods are eaten, so that Passover is experienced long before its abstract ideas are taught. Children eat the matzo and the bitter horseradish (symbolizing the bitterness of slavery) and drink the four cups of wine year after year, and only later are they told, "This is why we do this." Before, during, and after the meal, we read the story of enslavement and liberation from the Haggadah (the word means "the telling"). A place is set at the Seder table for the prophet Elijah, and at one point we open the door to welcome him. According to the biblical legend, Elijah never died but went up to heaven alive in a fiery chariot. He has thus come to serve as a "commuter" between heaven and earth, privy to the secret knowledge of heaven. We believe that one day he will come to announce the

* More than a thousand years after the Exodus, the early Christians worked a similar religious alchemy on the pagan birth-and-fertility holiday of the early spring, with its symbols of eggs and rabbits, celebrating the rebirth of natural life after the winter, turning it into a celebration of the return to life of the crucified Christ. Jesus was now the lamb whose blood on the wooden cross, resembling the doorpost of the Exodus story, would deliver his followers from spiritual, rather than physical, slavery.

imminent arrival of the Messiah and the delivery of the world from all imperfection. That is why, at the last synagogue service of each of the pilgrim festivals, the *haftarah,* the reading from the prophets, is a vision of messianic redemption. On Passover, for example, it is Isaiah's vision of the wolf lying down with the lamb. It is our way of saying: "Before this year is out, before this holiday comes around again, may the final redemption have come and may the world have become what God wants it to be."

The youngest child at the Seder asks the Four Questions ("Why is this night so different from all other nights? Why do we eat matzo, bite the bitter herb, dip our food in salt water?") and the leader of the Seder answers by telling the biblical story of the Exodus, explaining the matzo and all the other unusual symbolic foods. The custom of spilling off several drops of wine recalls how innocent Egyptians had to suffer because of their ruler's stubbornness. Our cup cannot be full as we empathize with them. (In our home, as in many others, we don't simply read the Haggadah but use its familiar passages to simulate a discussion of the Passover themes of life, liberation, sacrifice, and gratitude.) Songs are sung, wine is drunk, children get drowsy as the evening wears on. It is all so different from the usual rushed suppers of the rest of the year. Most Jewish children, for whom synagogue services are interchangeable and unintelligible, grow up with warm memories of going to grandparents' homes for the long, exotic Passover meal. Young couples feel they have turned a corner in their marriage the first year they invite the in-laws for a Seder meal instead of going to them.

Like much of Judaism, Passover happens mostly in the home. Surveys show that the Passover Seder is the single most observed tradition in all of Judaism, not so much for its theological message but because it is a family occasion, a time for people coming together over good food and good feelings.

The Seder meal is observed on the first two evenings of Passover. The holiday, with its special prayers and foods, continues for eight days (seven days in Israel and in the Reform tradition). But its message of God siding with the oppressed against the powerful, its account of God freeing Israel from human bondage so that we could serve Him, continues to reverberate throughout the year.

Shavuot/Pentecost, the Feast of Weeks

Shavuot, the third of the pilgrim festivals, is an anomaly. Theoretically, it is just as important as Sukkot and Pesach. Thematically, as the anniversary of the giving of the Torah, it should be a major festival. But somehow it has become the most neglected important day of the Jewish year. In the Talmud, Rosh HaShanah, Yom Kippur, Sukkot, Pesach, and even Purim each have their own tractate, spelling out the laws of observing the holiday. Shavuot has none. In the contemporary world, Hanukkah and Pesach give Jewish families sacred occasions to observe while our Christian neighbors are celebrating Christmas and Easter. Shavuot comes in early June when there are no parallel holidays in the non-Jewish world. And it may be that the message of Passover—"You're not going to be slaves anymore"—is more appealing than the message of Shavuot: "But you have to live this rigorous, demanding life instead."

What is this holiday that deserves to be better known and more widely celebrated than it is? Shavuot, like the other two pilgrim festivals, was originally a farmers' holiday. Seven weeks after the wheat ripened in early spring, the first fruits would ripen on the trees. The farmer would offer them to God with a prayer of thanks, not only for the fact that Nature had done its work again but as an articulation of gratitude that this descendant of slaves had his own land to tend and could feed his family with its produce.

After the biblical period, the sages noticed that the revelation at Sinai took place seven weeks after the Exodus, so the two themes of

Revelation and harvest were combined into a single holiday, with the same blend of agricultural gratitude and moral-historical awareness we have noted in the other pilgrimage occasions. Shavuot became the anniversary of the Revelation of the Torah. In many synagogues, it is marked today by Confirmation services, in which adolescents, after three years of study following Bar Mitzvah, pledge themselves to live by the Torah, thus not only reading about but reenacting the Covenant at Sinai. There is also a growing custom of recognizing the presence of converts to Judaism, individual men and women who have experienced in their own lives what the rest of us can only read about, the experience of personally accepting the Torah even as the Jews at Sinai did. Appropriately, one of the featured scriptural readings on Shavuot is the Book of Ruth, whose heroine is a convert to Judaism, a Moabite woman who is drawn to join the people of Israel because of the kindness they show her. (Legend has it that one rabbi, fastening on the themes of Confirmation, Torah, Revelation, and honoring converts, gave a sermon describing Shavuot as the "holiday of youth, truth, and Ruth.")

Two other Shavuot customs deserve mention. The practice originated among medieval Jewish mystics, and has become popular in recent years, of staying up all night, or at least till midnight, reading through the entire Torah (or in some traditions, reading a section from each of the five books), so that we are reenacting the experience of our ancestors. (The story is told of a five-year-old girl who heard the legend that if you look up into the sky at midnight on Shavuot, you can see God and anything you ask for will be granted. She begged her parents to let her stay up till midnight. They refused, but offered a compromise. "You can't stay up that late when you're only five. Wait until you're ten, and we'll let you stay up till midnight and look for God." The girl shook her head. "No! When I'm ten, I won't believe it anymore.")

And there is a custom of eating cheese and other dairy foods on Shavuot. It probably has to do with the warm summer weather, but a charming legend explains that when the Israelites heard the rules of the Torah, including the dietary laws, they were embarrassed by their nonkosher dishes, discarded them all, and ate only simple foods for the rest of the holiday.

The twentieth-century Jewish philosopher Franz Rosenzweig has written that God interacts with this world in three ways: as Creator (God's relating to the world of Nature, fashioning it and setting it in motion), as Revealer (God's relating to humanity, summoning them to live by His will and leading them to understand what that represents), and as Redeemer (God's bringing the realm of Nature and the realm of human beings into perfect harmony with each other, bringing about the ideal state of the Kingdom of God on Earth). The three pilgrim festivals represent those three modes of interaction. On Sukkot, the harvest festival amidst the beauty of the world in autumn, we encounter God the Creator, God as manifest in the beauty, power, and order of Nature, the earth that yields its harvest. On Shavuot, the Torah festival, we encounter the God of Revelation, who shared His Torah with us at Sinai. And on Pesach, as we recall the redemption from Egypt with which the story of the Jewish people began, we celebrate God the Redeemer and look forward to the final redemption.

One more calendar note: In Orthodox and Conservative congregations outside the land of Israel, each festival day (Shavuot, and the first and last days of Sukkot and Pesach) is celebrated for two days. The beginning of the lunar month was based on visual sighting of the new moon in Jerusalem. In an age when communication between countries was slow, Jews living outside Israel could never be sure if the moon had been sighted in Jerusalem before or after sunset on the day when they saw it emerge. To make sure that they did not inadvertently treat a holy day as an ordinary day, they would observe both the earlier date and the day following. In Israel and in Reform congregations, only one day is observed.

Purim, Hanukkah, Tisha B'Av

These three occasions mark historical events that occurred after the time of the Torah, so their observance is less solemn and less fully spelled out by Jewish law. Purim is the quintessential holiday of Jewish vulnerability. It tells the story of how the Jews of Persia, though loyal and innocent, faced persecution and extermination, and were saved only by the courage of one woman and by a series of fortunate coincidences. The holiday recalls the events that took place around the year 500 B.C. as described in the biblical Book of Esther. Haman, the wicked prime minister of the far-flung Persian empire, convinced his gullible king that his Jewish subjects were a threat to his kingdom because their rules and customs were different from those of other Persians. The king agreed to have them killed and their wealth confiscated, but his favorite queen, Esther, who was Jewish, saved the day with a personal appeal to the king. This Arabian Nights tale of danger and delivery is recalled with merrymaking, costumes, food, and wine, including the obligation to get so drunk that one cannot keep track of who are the good guys and who are the bad guys. (What other religion has a holiday on which you are obliged to get drunk, and some people refuse to do so on the grounds that they are not religious? And is it only a coincidence that Purim, coming a month before Passover, in so many ways resembles the Carnival-Mardi Gras celebrations before the Lenten season and its anticipation of Easter?) One commentator has observed that the mood of the pilgrim festivals is one of joy, while the mood of Purim is one of fun. There is room in life for both.

Hanukkah is second only to Passover as the most widely observed Jewish holiday, not because of its own importance but because it comes in late December, when our neighbors and our entire culture are caught up in celebrating Christmas. Hanukkah thus becomes "the Jewish Christmas," giving us something to do in affirmation of our Jewish identity and a way of making our children feel less deprived. It is a misleading comparison, as out of balance as the December musical program in which Handel's *Messiah* is followed by "I Have a Little Dreidel," because Christmas is a fundamental Christian occasion while Hanukkah is perhaps the sixth or seventh most important occasion of the Jewish year.

But how many people know that if it were not for Hanukkah, there would be no Christmas? In the second century B.C., the land of Israel was a province of the Greek empire, divided up and presided over by the successors of Alexander the

Great. The emperor tried to use religion to unify his subjects in their several provinces by prohibiting all local religions and compelling all to join in the worship of the Greek gods (with a little emperor-worship thrown in for good measure). Most people went along with the edict; the ancient assumption was that if somebody conquered you, his gods must be more powerful than your gods. Only the Jews, with their commitment to freedom and their stubborn insistence that their God was the only God, resisted. Though vastly outnumbered, they fought a guerrilla campaign so effective that the Greeks gave in and let them have their religious freedom. The Temple of Jerusalem, which had been turned into a Greek shrine, was cleansed and rededicated to Jewish worship, and the Eternal Light, which had been extinguished, was lit again. (The word *Hanukkah* means "dedication.") Had the Jews not rebelled against the Greeks in the year 165 B.C., had they disappeared into Greek culture as so many Near Eastern people did, Jewish history would have ended then and there. We would have been forgotten like the Hittites and Ammonites. There would have been no Jewish community for Jesus to be born into a century and a half later. No one would have remembered the messianic promises he claimed to fulfill. Without Hanukkah, there would have been no Christmas.

Hanukkah is observed by lighting one candle the first night, two on the second, and so on, until eight candles are burning in the menorah on the eighth and final night. Coming at the darkest time of the year, it brings a message of hope to the oppressed and to the depressed. It brings the message of light winning out over darkness, the message that even a little light can dispel a lot of darkness.

Tisha B'Av is a fast day (not nearly as well known as Yom Kippur) that occurs every summer and commemorates the destruction of the Temple of Jerusalem at the hands of the Babylonians. King Solomon, David's son and successor, built the Temple around the year 950 B.C., making Jerusalem the religious as well as the political capital of his country. Three hundred sixty years later, the Babylonians destroyed Jerusalem and exiled its inhabitants. The city fell, after a long and terrible battle, on the ninth day of the month Av, and Jews mourned its fall by fasting annually on that anniversary.

A generation later, some of the exiles returned to Jerusalem and rebuilt the Temple on its original site. This second Temple stood for about six hundred years, and by ominous coincidence was destroyed in a war against Rome, falling again on the ninth day of Av. Over the centuries, the day has become a time for recalling all the suffering and the vulnerability of the Jewish people in exile.

Why do some Jews still fast today for an event that happened nearly twenty-six centuries ago? Partly because to be a Jew is to be a "prisoner of memory," to cherish the glory and the pain of the biblical past as if they had happened to us, not only to some remote ancestor of ours. Most Americans tend to be impatient with history, eager to forget about something as soon as it is over. Jews tend to cherish history, even when what we remember is painful or embarrassing. History, after all, is where we met God and saw His purposes worked out.

A second reason was given long ago by the prophet Zechariah, who lived in the early days of the second Temple. People asked him why they still had to mourn and fast for Solomon's Temple, now that it had been restored. He answered that what we grieve for on Tisha B'Av is not just a building. We grieve for all those tendencies in the human soul that cause men to go to war, so that cities are destroyed and their inhabitants killed. Jerusalem may be restored, but that pain still endures.

Yom HaShoah, Yom HaAtzmaut, Yom Yerushalayim

My generation has seen three new days of observance added to the Jewish calendar, the first such additions in two thousand years. Twelve days after the Passover Seder, we pause to commemorate the six million victims of Hitler's brutality.*

How was the date chosen? In the spring of 1943, only a few thousand of what had been the great and proud world of Polish Jewry remained alive in the Warsaw ghetto. As Passover approached, with its message of divinely aided liberation, the remaining Jews decided to die fighting the Germans rather than waiting to be killed. With a few weapons they had smuggled in, they rose in revolt against the military force that had conquered all of Europe. They did significant damage to the Nazis in Warsaw before their rebellion was put down and the remaining Jews killed. The twenty-seventh day of the Hebrew month Nisan was the day the revolt began. As Jews began to realize they needed to commemorate the Shoah as much as they needed to

* Though the word *Holocaust* has become the universally recognized term for Hitler's war against the Jews, I have always felt a measure of discomfort with it. *Holocaust* is a biblical term for the offering on the altar that is completely consumed by fire and goes up to heaven in smoke. I am not comfortable with the notion of Hitler's victims as a sacrifice offered to God. They were not sacrificed; they were murdered by brutal sadists who cared not at all for the biblical God. Modern Hebrew uses the term *Shoah,* the Calamity, to refer to the fate of European Jews under the Nazis.

commemorate the destruction of Solomon's Temple, lest all that cruelty and all that bravery be forgotten, they settled on that date, the date of the Warsaw ghetto uprising, as the annual commemoration. It is our way of saying that what we want to remember about the Nazi epoch is not only the image of the suffering Jew, the Jew as victim, but the image of the Jew as the one who stood for humanity in the face of brutality.

Two and a half years after the war ended, the United Nations voted to divide Palestine into two separate states, one for its Jewish inhabitants, another for its Arab residents. (The U.N. had done the same in India, in Korea, in Vietnam, and everywhere where the withdrawal of colonial or occupying powers left two competing populations unwilling to share power with each other.) For the first time in eighteen centuries, we Jews had a land of our own. The unmatched importance of this event for the Jewish soul is the subject of an entire chapter later in this book. But every year since 1948, Jews of every religious and political orientation have celebrated Yom HaAtzmaut, the anniversary of modern Israel. When we recite the prayer authorized by the Israeli Rabbinate, referring to Israel as "the beginning of the flowering of our redemption," we are saying that the return of the Jewish people to its ancestral land is not just another political phenomenon. It is an event of universal spiritual meaning, a development that has the fingerprints of God on it.

The celebration of Israel's independence comes annually three weeks after Passover, and barely a week after Yom HaShoah. The juxtaposition of dates has led many people to see a relationship: Israel as God's (or the world's) compensation to the Jewish people for the Shoah. For me, there can be no compensation for the Shoah. The only relationship I will acknowledge (beyond speculating on the guilty consciences of some politicians) is that the establishing of Israel testifies to the vitality of the Jewish people even after the incomparable bloodletting of the Holocaust.

Those of you who are old enough to remember the events of the Six-Day War in June 1967 will recall how we trembled for the well-being of Israel in the days before the war, and how we responded to Israel's stunning victory with the indescribable relief of someone who has stared disaster in the face and emerged unharmed. Nonreligious Jews were surprised to discover how deeply they cared about Israel, and how thrilled they were when the religious sites of Old Jerusalem, which had been occupied by the Jordanians for nineteen years, were returned to Jewish hands. The custom has begun to emerge of marking the anniversary of that victory, the twenty-eighth day of Iyar (the month after Nisan), as Yom Yerushalayim, Jerusalem Day, and acknowledging the hand of God in that miraculous triumph, even as our ancestors saw the hand of God in their crossing of the Red Sea.

I am told that there is a Chinese curse "May you live in interesting times." Any Jew, any person who has lived in the last half of the twentieth century, has lived in interesting times, and it has often been painful and problematic. We have learned a lot—too much, perhaps—about man's capacity for cruelty, and we have learned much about the incredible resiliency of the human spirit, its capacity to survive and transcend that cruelty. We have learned to see the hand of God, not so much in the Calamity as in the ability of survivors to affirm the value of life, and the value of being Jewish, even in the shadow of the Calamity. And to ensure that we never forget those lessons, we have expanded the Jewish calendar to include them.

When I was an army chaplain, I would periodically have to inform the post commander of upcoming Jewish holidays so that Jewish personnel would be excused to attend services. The standard phrase used to describe the holidays of any religious tradition was "days of religious obligation." I was never comfortable with that phrase. For me, the red-letter days of the Jewish calendar were not days of religious obligation; they were days of religious opportunity. Fifty-two times a year, the Sabbath gives us the opportunity to step off the treadmill of economic striving and scheduling pressures, and redefine ourselves as free men and women, and as members of a family. Every fall, the Jewish calendar offers us days of solemn majesty, days of cleansing and reconciliation, days of remembering to be grateful for the good things of the earth and world. Every winter, Hanukkah summons us to light candles to chase the darkness. Every spring, Pesach comes with its Seder meals, with its food, wine, family memories, and message of liberation. Seventy-six times a year, the Jewish calendar calls on us to stop defining ourselves by what we do for a living or what we fill our days with, and asks us to define ourselves by who we are and who we might be.

5

What We Believe About God

*T*O THIS POINT, we have spoken about many things, about Sabbaths and holidays, about food laws and rules governing proper speech, but we have not said very much about God. This may surprise you, because many people think that when you study a religion, the first thing you have to learn is what it believes and teaches about God. But the religion I know best, Judaism, stresses ethics and community, the effort to become fully human as you relate to the people around you, more than it stresses the nature of God.

And yet, when we talk about Judaism, it is clear that God has to be a part, the most important part, of that conversation. God gives us the ability to be human, and summons us to live up to our human potential. He has brought us to understand what we need to do to be fully human. It is God's concern for us that invests our every act with significance. Without that God-dimension, the issue of how people treat each other would be a matter of good manners rather than morality. Without the faith that God underwrites our understanding of right and wrong, the idea that the world belongs to the strongest and the most ruthless would be as valid a rule to live by as "love your neighbor as yourself."

To understand and appreciate Judaism, we have to talk about God, His existence, His nature, the extent of His knowledge of the future, and the question of where God's power ends and human freedom begins. We have to talk about God, even though our limited human minds can comprehend God only in a limited way and cannot even put into words everything we comprehend. We have to talk about Him, even at the risk of appearing arrogant in our claims that we understand Him, because it is the presence of God in Jewish history that gives significance to the story of the Jewish people and the lives of Jews today.

But how shall we talk about God? There is a strange passage in the Book of Exodus (chapter 33, verses 18-23), right after the incident of the Golden Calf, in which the Israelites who had stood at Sinai angered God by worshipping an idol and Moses had to intercede and plead for divine forgiveness. Moses says to God, "Let me behold Your presence," that is, "Let me get to know You face-to-face, instead of only through verbal revelations. If

I am going to persuade the Israelites to worship and revere You, and not have any more lapses like the one with the Golden Calf, I have to know more about who and what You are." God answers, "No man can see Me and live, but hide here in the cleft of the rock as I pass by. You will be able to see My back but not My face."

What are we to make of that statement, that Moses will be able to see God's back though not His face? I cannot take it literally, that one can see God's back. I take it to mean that we cannot see God directly but we can see God-in-action. We can see the difference God makes as He passes through the world. Just as we cannot see the wind, but can only see things blown by the wind and know that the wind is real and powerful; just as we cannot see electricity, but can only see things activated by electricity; just as we cannot see love, but can see people behaving differently, being braver and more caring because they love; so we cannot see God. We can only see His aftereffects.

Earlier in the Book of Exodus, there is a similar conversation between God and Moses, which teaches us something about the biblical notion of God and how hard it is to say anything definitive about Him. It takes place at the Burning Bush, the first time that God speaks to Moses. He summons him to confront Pharaoh and demand that the Hebrew slaves go free. Moses responds (Exodus 3:13) by asking God, "What is Your name?" It may be hard for the modern reader to understand the point of that question. Moses is not changing the subject and saying, "Excuse me, what was Your name? I didn't get it the first time." In ancient times, a name was more than an identifying label. Your name was your essence, what you were all about, your identity rather than just your identification. To ask "What is God's name?" is to ask "What is God all about? What does He stand for?"

God answers Moses enigmatically in three Hebrew words which defy simple translation, *EHYEH ASHER EHYEH.* The usual translation is "I am that I am" or "I will be what I will be," both of which are about as obscure as the Hebrew original. The phrase has been explained philosophically to mean that God is pure Being (whatever that means). It has been taken as indicating God's arbitrariness, the idea that He cannot be comprehended by human minds ("I will be whatever I choose to be, and don't try to figure Me out"). Another interpretation persuasively notes that the word *Ehyeh* appears in the verse just before Moses' question, with God saying to Moses, "When you stand before Pharaoh, I will be [*Ehyeh*] with you." In other words, God is seen as saying to Moses, "Don't ask about My essence, My nature. That is too private, too Other for you to know and understand. Ask instead about the difference I can make in your life. When you have to do something difficult [like confronting Pharaoh or changing bad habits], *I will be* with you to help you in your struggle."

In the rest of the Bible and subsequent Jewish literature, God's personal Name is Yhwh (grammatically the same word as *Ehyeh,* but in third person rather than first person: *He is,* rather than *I am*). It is a word so holy, so intimate, that Jews would not pronounce it, substituting terms like "the Lord," "the Name," "the Holy One." Only once a year, on Yom Kippur, the Day of Atonement, would the High Priest, officiating at the Temple in Jerusalem, call upon God by His holy Name to forgive His people. For any other human being at any other time, to use that Name would be an unforgivable presumption of familiarity with God, presuming to be on a first-name basis with Him, as it were.

We cannot understand God's Name, any more than we can understand God. But it may mean any or all of the following:

—God is.

—God is more than we can comprehend.

—God is with us in our efforts to do that which is right and hard.

And one more thing: look at those Names as

they are spoken in the original Hebrew—*Ehyeh, Yhwh.* Do you notice something unusual about them? They have virtually no consonants. The *Y*'s and *H*'s don't interrupt the flow of sound the way most consonants would. They are almost pure sound, almost like breathing. Just as God created the animals by saying, "Let there be . . .," but brought Adam to life by *breathing* into him, putting a bit of the divine breath into him, God is seen as the breath of life. Just as the invisible air around us makes it biologically possible for us to live, so the invisible presence of God, breathed into us at birth and reinforced every time we encounter the Divine Name, makes it possible for us to function as human beings. And at the end of our human existence, when we die, what happens? God–*Yhwh* reclaims the divine gift of breath.

When we talk about what we as Jews believe about God, we must remind ourselves of Rule One: Some Jews believe certain things, other Jews believe differently, and there is no central authority to declare one group correct and the other in error. This is partly because of the relatively minor role that theology plays in Judaism: God is important; talking about God is not all that important. But it is mostly because statements about God are not really so much about God as they are about us. To say that God heals the sick is not a statement about what activities fill God's schedule. It is a way of saying that when we have been sick and we recover, we have experienced God in our lives (not His face but His works). To say that God forgives is not a comment on God's emotional state but a recognition of our own ability to feel cleansed of guilt because God is real in the world. To say that God hears prayer does not describe God's auditory system; it answers the question of whether or not praying is a waste of time. Statements about God, then, do not describe God (how could we ever dare to do that?). They describe how we and our world are different because of God. An old rabbinic text reads, "God is like a mirror. The mirror never changes, but everyone who looks at it sees a different face." One might say that the Jewish concept of God is largely an idealized vision of how an authentic human being, fashioned in God's image, would behave. As the sages of the Talmud put it, "Just as God heals the sick, so should you heal the sick. Just as He sustains the poor, you should sustain the poor. Just as He comforts the grieving and forgives those who disappoint Him, so should you do as well."

This then is one person's summary, born out of a lifetime of study, reflection, and teaching, of what Judaism says about God. I can guarantee that it will perplex some people and upset others. it attempts not to answer the question "Who or what is God?"

but to answer the question "When is God?"—that is, what has to be happening to us and around us for us to recognize the presence of God?

Does God exist? Moses Maimonides, the greatest intellect and the greatest philosopher the Jewish people has ever produced (he lived in twelfth-century Spain and North Africa), taught that when we use human language to talk about God, we are being poetic, metaphorical. God is so totally Other that we cannot describe Him with words borrowed from descriptions of human beings. But we must talk about God, we must strive to understand Him and His role in our lives, and we have no other words. Maimonides went on to say that we can speak accurately (as opposed to metaphorically) about God only when we speak negatively, when we deny inaccurate statements about God. To say that "God exists" does not explain anything about God; it denies that God is a figment of our imagination, a useful fiction to make people feel better, like Santa Claus or the Tooth Fairy. To say that "God hears our prayers" does not say anything about God; it rejects the idea that praying is a waste of time. And to affirm that there is only one God is a way of denying that there are many gods. If there were many gods, we could not speak of the Divine Will for goodness; what one god permitted, another would forbid. What was good in the sight of one would be evil by another's standards.

For the biblical mind, the existence of God was too obvious to require a statement of faith. It would be like debating whether the sun exists or whether it gets dark at night. The Bible commands us to love God, to fear (that is, to revere) God, to obey God, to trust God, and to sanctify His name in the sight of the world by our behavior. It never commands us to believe in Him.

There is one passage in the Torah that discusses believing in God, and it is a monumentally important one. But what is at issue there is not God's existence but His reliability. The reference comes in chapter 15 of Genesis. Abraham complains to God: "You said I would be the father of a great nation, but I am an old man and my wife and I are still childless." God directs Abraham to look up to heaven and tells him, "See how many stars there are; your descendants will be that numerous." We then read that "Abraham believed in God, and God deemed him righteous for doing so" (Genesis 15:6). What does it mean for Abraham to believe in God in that context? God's existence is not the issue. Abraham has just been talking to Him. At issue is God's reliability; will He do what He has promised to do? To believe in God is not to affirm His existence, but to trust Him, to give Him the benefit of the doubt, to believe that what should happen but has not yet happened will eventually happen. This is the act of righteousness, the favor, that Abraham (and we) can do for God.

Think of it this way: A woman is married to a man whose job requires him to travel frequently. Friends say to her, "Aren't you worried about what he is doing all those nights when he's away from you?" She answers, "I believe in my husband." When she says that, she is not stating that her husband exists (who would challenge that?). She is saying that he is a person of integrity who lives up to his commitments. Similarly, when Jews say that they believe in God, it is not His existence but His reliability that we are affirming.

For the Psalmist, the issue is not whether God *exists* but whether God *cares.* When we read in Psalm 14, "The fool says in his heart, There is no God," the real issue is whether God takes note of what humans do, whether He intervenes in our affairs. Do bad people get away with murder because God is too remote to notice or get involved? And again, that question is not really about God; it is about us. "Does God care whether we do good or evil?" is not a question about God's emotional involvement. It is a way of asking, "Do our choices matter? Does the content of our lives have any real significance?" For the biblical mind, an atheist is not a person who philosophically denies the existence of God.

An atheist is a person who denies the ethical significance of human beings, saying, "People are just animals obeying instincts; it makes no moral difference what they do."

What does God demand from us? As I have suggested, God wants us to choose goodness, to exercise our uniquely human power to sanctify the world. He doesn't expect us to be perfect, but He expects us to be serious about our lives. I have never understood those theologies that picture God as waiting to catch us in a single mistake and send us to hell. I find myself wondering what sort of parents those theologians must have had, that they picture God that way. For me, the notion of "God watching" makes me think more of the child learning to ride a bicycle, calling out to her mother, "Watch me!" so that the mother will take pride in her achievements and will be available to pick her up if she should fall.

What about heaven and hell? Over the centuries, many Jews have believed in heaven as a reward for the righteous, especially the righteous who have been shortchanged in this life. As a general rule, the harder life was for Jews in this world, the more attractive the belief in a happy afterlife tended to become. Few Jews have believed in hell. One would have to ascribe too much sadism, too much of a delight in punishing, to God, and while we believe God stands for justice and while sometimes getting even with bad people can be a godly act, we would like to think God is above the sort of vindictiveness some hellfire preachers ascribe to Him.

My own preference is to follow Maimonides, who suggested that, when a righteous person dies, his reward is that his soul is freed from its earthly body and gets to spend eternity in the presence of God. When a wicked person dies, he is denied that incomparable reward. Who needs hell? Being denied God's company is punishment enough.

Is God all-knowing and all-powerful? At one level, these questions are word games. I have heard skeptics mockingly ask, "Can God create a rock so heavy that even He can't lift it?" Whether you answer yes or no, you are left saying that there is something God can't do. (The real answer, by the way, is that a rock so heavy that an all-powerful deity can't lift it is a logically impossible, self-contradictory construct, like a four-sided triangle. It is not a limitation of God's power to say that He cannot do the logically impossible.) My own position is that the word *omnipotent,* or *all-powerful,* is a philosophical term, not a religious one. Its goal is philosophical consistency, not reverence. I find a religious answer in the Bible, where I meet a God who is awesomely powerful but not all-controlling.

Readers of my generation may remember kryptonite. As a child, I followed the adventures of Superman on the radio and in the comics. The problem was that Superman, with his great strength, speed, and X-ray vision, would always win and could never be harmed. Where then would the suspense come from? It would be like watching a football game between the Super Bowl champions and a local high school team. So Superman's creators invented kryptonite, a substance whose presence made Superman weak and vulnerable. Without that, there could be no drama.

What is the biblical equivalent of kryptonite, the substance that limits God's power? I find two areas: God does not suspend laws of Nature, and God gives human beings free will to choose good or evil, life or death (even as He urges us, but cannot compel us, to choose life).

Consider, for example, the passage in Deuteronomy 20:5–7. When the Israelites are mustered for war, the leaders are to say to them: Any man who has built a new house and not yet moved into it, betrothed a wife and not yet married her, planted a vineyard and not yet drunk its wine— let him go home and be safe, lest he die in battle and never complete what he has begun. Now, if God controls everything that happens in the world, why not let those men go into battle and count on God to bring them home safely? In fact, why not put them in the front lines, relying on God's mercy and sense of fairness to protect them? Apparently, even the Book of Deuteronomy, which more than any other biblical text speaks of God's rewarding the righteous and punishing the wicked, recognizes that some things are out of God's control.

Laws of Nature are one form of biblical kryptonite. Nature may be beautiful and orderly but it is morally blind. Falling rocks and speeding bullets obey laws of physics, irrespective of what harm they may do to innocent people in their path. The sages of the Talmud put it this way: If a man steals seeds and plants them, it would be morally fitting if the stolen seeds would refuse to grow. But the world of Nature follows its course, and the seeds grow. If a woman is raped, it would be morally better for her not to become pregnant and have to bear the rapist's child. That is not how God wants children to be conceived. But the world of Nature is not moral, and sometimes the unfortunate victim does become pregnant, because laws of Nature do not always carry out God's will.

The other source of "kryptonite" consists of human beings exercising their free will in selfish, destructive ways. Without that freedom to choose, as we have said, people could not do good unless they could also be bad. And in the process, inno-cent people get hurt, and we must believe that God is as outraged by it as you and I are.

The Bible makes a claim about God that is perhaps more audacious than the claim that He is all-powerful. It says that He has the power to turn human evil into good. In the biblical story of the children of Jacob, Joseph's brothers are jealous of him and sell him into slavery. He finds himself first a servant, then a prisoner in Egypt. Through a series of events, he rises to become Pharaoh's adviser on distributing food in time of famine. Joseph's brothers come to buy food from this powerful official whom they do not recognize, and after testing them to be sure that they have grown and changed, Joseph reveals his identity to them. He says to them "You intended to do me harm, but the Lord turned it into good, that I might save many lives" (Genesis 50:20). In other words, God did not want the brothers to sell Joseph into slavery, but He could not prevent them from doing so once they chose to do it. What God could do was to provide the spiritual alchemy to transform Joseph's personal misfor-tune into something life-sustaining. Rather than prevent Joseph from suffering unfairly (He would have had to cancel the brothers' moral freedom to do that), He guided Joseph to turn that suffering into something redemptive.

I have experienced that power of God's in my own life. When my wife and I learned that our three-year-old son had an incurable illness that would cause him to die young, I could not accept the notion that God wanted this bright, innocent child to suffer and die. But I could believe that, in the face of genetic misfortune, God could give us the strength to cope, to survive and ultimately transcend the tragedy. Unable to keep my son from dying, God showed me how to redeem his death from being a statistic and forge it into a book that would bring healing to millions.

And I have seen other people experience God's transforming power in similar ways—the divorced wife who comes to see what happened to her not as a rejection, but as a liberation that frees her to become a more independent and authentic person; the therapist who uses her own painful life experiences to develop a sense of compassion for her patients that no amount of reading could have given her. They all echo the words of Joseph: You intended to do me harm, but the Lord showed me how to turn it into something good and life-sustaining.

A Protestant theologian of my acquaintance, David Griffin, once said to me, "I believe God's power is unlimited. But His power is not the power to control, it is the power to enable." God does not make things turn out according to His will. He gives us the ability to know His will, and the dedication to bring it about, if that is what *we* choose to do. God will cure cancer, for example, not by deciding one day "Okay, that's it, no more malignant tumors," but by giving human beings the intelligence and the caring to find a cure.

I said to him, "David, that's a wonderful insight. Now I understand why, in the Bible and in so many other religious texts, God is pictured as fire. [Think of the Burning Bush, Mount Sinai, the Eternal Light.] Fire is not an object. Fire is the process of releasing the energy concealed in a lump of coal or a piece of wood. This is what God does. He releases the energy hidden in every one of us."

In the interests of fairness, I must concede that a great many Jews, including many Jewish theologians, believe that God is all-powerful, that He controls everything that happens in the world, and if we cannot understand His decisions, the limitations are ours, not His. What impresses me is not that Jewish thinkers differ so strongly on such a fundamental question, but that, realizing how sharply we differ, we have so little trouble praying together and recognizing each other as adherents of the same faith.

Does God know the future before it happens? And if He does, how can we be held responsible for the choices we make, if they were foreordained? There are three types of answers traditionally given to this question. One asserts that the more information you have about a situation, the more likely you are to know what will happen. People who run airlines know six months in advance how many people are likely to fly from Boston to Chicago on a Tuesday afternoon and plan their schedules accordingly, before the travelers have begun to think about their trips. Gamblers calculate the winner of a football game, and are often right, before the game is played. Teachers can often predict which students will do well on a test, which ones will do poorly, and which ones will find a reason to be absent. Presumably, the more clever these observers are and the more accurate information they are given, the more likely they are to predict correctly, without in any way diminishing the freedom of the subjects to choose to do or not do what the observer guessed they would. And presumably, since God is wiser and better informed than any of us, He can predict even more accurately.

But there is a difference between *knowing* the future and *correctly guessing* the future, and the champions of God's omniscience (another of those Greek words that philosophers use; it means "all-knowing") would insist that God *knows* the future, not that He makes a well-informed guess about it. He is less like a sports handicapper and more like the director of a movie who knows what the ending will be while the audience sits in suspense. But if God knows how the story will end, are we then free to choose what we will do?

So let me offer another interpretation, one that may be a bit hard to follow: We live in a time-bound world, in which the past has already happened and the future is ahead of us. But God, who created time, stands outside time. Past, present, and future are all simultaneous for Him. Terms like *already, not yet, before it happens* don't apply to God. Not being God, not being able to escape from our time-bound frame of reference, we can't understand what it means for past, present, and future to be simultaneous, any more than a two-dimensional figure in a painting can imagine himself moving around and looking behind objects in the painting. Think of yourself looking at a comic strip in the Sunday paper. From your point of view, outside the strip, you can see what happens in the first panel, the fourth panel, and the eighth panel at the same time. But for the characters in the comic strip, those events happen one after another. That may be what it is like for God to look at our behavior, which to us happens over the course of time, and know the end at the beginning.

Or yet another way of looking at it: I would remind the reader of Maimonides' warning that when we use terms of human discourse to describe God, the words don't fit Him the way they fit us. God may "know" the future, but His knowledge is different from our "knowing" the outcome of a sporting event. Perhaps statements about God's knowing the future are really statements about how *we* perceive the world as it unfolds. God's providence (the word, by the way, literally means "seeing ahead") reveals itself in the discovery that, when we do something or when something happens to us, the spiritual means we require to deal with what has just happened are already prepared and waiting for us, *as if* God knew what was going to happen and provided (from the same root as *providence*) what we would need to deal with it.

Why does God permit evil? This is probably the most troubling God-question of all: What is God's role in all the suffering and tragedy that mars the world? It deserves more than a two-page answer, and in fact I have written a book (*When Bad Things Happen to Good People*) devoted solely to this issue. Basically, Jewish responses have taken two forms.

Historically, many sages have had to admit that we cannot understand God's ways because we cannot see things from God's point of view. We can't know all the facts, and we can't see the long-term results down the road. Sometimes they say that God knows what is best for us better than we do. (I think of all the people I know who were deeply depressed when they lost their jobs, only to tell me six months later, "You know, that was the best thing that ever happened to me. It was the wrong job for me and I didn't have the nerve to leave it on my own." I think too of the country music song about the man who, as an adult, runs into the woman who had been his high school sweetheart. He remembers praying to God every night to make her love him, and wondering why God never did what he so fervently asked for. Now, meeting her as an adult, he concludes, "Some of God's greatest gifts are unanswered prayers.") Sometimes the sages simply shrug their shoulders in bafflement and say that our task is not to understand and explain God but to trust Him and follow Him.

I don't find that a satisfactory answer. Faced with so much suffering on the part of good people, I cannot be satisfied with a shrug. I need to know which side God is on: Are the accidents and crippling illnesses His doing? I find my answer in the limitations of God's power outlined above. Sometimes bad things happen to good people because laws of Nature can't tell a good person from a bad one, and sometimes they happen because God will not interfere to take away our human freedom, no matter how destructively we intend to use it.

Even something as monstrous as the Holocaust comes to be seen as Man's doing, not God's. "Why did God let it happen?" Because God determined at the outset that He would not compromise our human freedom to choose between good and evil, no matter how atrociously we misused it. If we didn't learn from history, from experience, from the voice of conscience, we would go on hurting and killing each other. "Couldn't God have made an exception to that rule in this one case, to save so many millions of lives?" I am not sure He could have, even if He had wanted to. But even if God theoretically could have intervened, would that mean He should also have intervened to stop Stalin and Pol Pot from killing millions of people in Russia and Cambodia? Or to keep other dictators from killing thousands? Or some madman with an assault rifle from killing dozens? If a human life is of infinite value, if the mother of an inner-city murder victim grieves for her dead child as deeply as the mother of a Holocaust victim does, on what grounds would God suspend the rules in one case and not in others? For me, the Holocaust is not a theological issue: "Why didn't God stop it?" For me, it is a psychological issue: "How could human beings have so grossly misused their freedom to decide how to treat each other?" It does not challenge my faith in God. If anything, it makes it harder for me to believe in man without God.

For those of us who cherish the notion of human freedom, not only as a solution to the question of God's role in tragedy but as one of the glories of the human condition, there is a passage in the Book of Exodus that we find troubling. It comes in the first part of the book, the narrative about God's freeing the Hebrew slaves from Egypt. God tells Moses that, in order to make it clear that the breakout to freedom is a miraculous deliverance and not the result of Pharaoh's generosity, He will "harden Pharaoh's heart" so that he will keep on refusing to let the slaves go until ten plagues have devastated his land and testified to God's saving power. Where is the fairness here, making Pharaoh do wrong and then punishing him for it? Does it imply that perhaps other people are cruel because God "hardened their hearts," and are not to be held responsible for it?

The best answer comes from the psychoanalyst Erich Fromm in his book *The Heart of Man,* and grows out of a close reading of the Exodus story. After several of the earlier plagues, we read that *Pharaoh hardens his own heart* (Exodus 8:11, 8:28)! Only after that do we read of God's hardening Pharaoh's heart (Exodus 9:12, 10:1, 10:20). From that, we learn a great and enduring lesson about human free will. We are free to choose how we will live and behave. But we can *give away that freedom* by the choices that we make. Every time we choose one path over another, we are choosing not only for that moment. We are shifting the odds as to how we will choose the next time we face that situation. For example, if we once cheat on our diet or falsify information on our income tax return, the next time we face that choice, we will not only have to deal with the same temptation again. We will have to deal with the memory of ourselves as a certain kind of person, a person who cheats or falsifies. A person can freely choose to become so dependent on drugs or alcohol, so bound to a certain habit that he can no longer freely choose whether to give it up or not.

Think of a person standing at a crossroads, having to choose between two alternative paths. For the moment, each of them is equally accessible. But every step taken down path A makes it easier to continue down path A and harder to turn back and choose path B. What was originally an even choice has now become an uneven one.

The first time Moses stood before him, Pharaoh could have said yes as easily as he could have said no. But every time he said no, he made it that much more likely that he would say no the next time as well. Not only did it become an issue of saving face and not admitting that he was wrong, he also had to deal with his own self-image as a person who says no to the slaves' demand for freedom.

Are people free to choose or does God force our hand? In the beginning, we are free, but with every wrong choice, we give away our freedom until in the end we may be telling the truth when we say, "I couldn't help it." But we would be wrong to blame God or to claim, "The Devil made me do it." Judaism has no need to invent a devil, when human weakness and selfishness do such a good job of explaining the messes we get into.

But of course, the process works the other way too. The first time we do something hard or brave, we have to force ourselves to do it. But the more often we do it, the more it becomes "second nature." The doubt, the uncertainty vanish; we come to think of ourselves as "the sort of person who does that." As the Talmud puts it, "The real reward for a good deed is that it makes the next good deed easier, and the real punishment for a sin is that it makes it more likely that you will commit the same sin the next time."

Is God a person? Is God male? A woman reader of my previous books complained to me about referring to God as "He." Do I believe that God is exclusively male? And if so, how can a woman avoid relating to God the way she relates to other powerful men in her life—with suspicion, with flirtation, with resentment?

When I try to think about God, I immediately confront a dilemma. I know that God is not really an old man who lives in the sky. I know that God is a different order of reality than I am. He is a source of energy and purpose and goodness, but has no physical body, no arms, no legs, no beard, no sexual organs. But I don't know how to think of God as real, except to think of Him as a person, even as I remind myself that I am being inaccurate as I do so. For me, God is not a person as you and I are. But He has personality in the sense that He stands for certain values, rather than being a blind, impersonal force like gravity.

God is personal in at least this sense: Some forces, like gravity and laws of physics, are impersonal. They treat us all alike. A person falling off the roof of a tall building will accelerate at a certain rate of speed irrespective of what kind of person he is and why he is falling. He can be old or young, married or single, virtuous or wicked. None of that will affect the question of how long it will take him to reach the ground.

But other forces, like love, courage, and healing, are personal. Each of us responds to them differently. They are filtered through the prism of our unique personality. God, as the author of love, courage, and healing, is personal to each of us in at least that sense. In the Bible, God is *grammatically* masculine ("May the Lord shine the light of *His* countenance upon you . . ."; even terms like *Lord* are specifically masculine). But *functionally* God is both male and female. Sometimes God acts like a father, laying down the law, demanding, summoning. And sometimes God acts like a mother, feeding, nurturing, protecting. In fact, there is at least one passage in the Midrash where God is pictured as a woman, and Moses is described as God's husband.

Ancient Hebrew, like English and other languages that evolved in a social setting where men monopolized power, bases its grammar on the assumption that men are the norm and nonmales are the deviation from that norm. Human beings are assumed to be men unless otherwise specified. ("We hold these truths to be self-evident, that all *men* are created equal." Sometimes, though rarely, being deviant from the norm can mean being superior to the ordinary, as in the military where restrooms used to be labeled "officers" and "men.") That this is unfair and demeaning to women, I will readily grant, but I don't know of a better alternative. To speak of God as "It" is to suggest a mechanical God, incapable of love, anger, or other human passions. To alternate gender ("Praise Him with timbrel and lyre, praise Her with loud-sounding cymbals"), in my opinion, serves only to draw excessive attention to the issue of God's gender. (In one congregation where they have rewritten the prayer book to alternate references to God as "Him" and "Her," one worshipper walked out, muttering, "They sound like a great couple.") One congregation I know of has rewritten the prayer book to refer to God only as "You," never as "He" or "Lord, King." That works well enough in prayer; I find it works less well in theological discussions. I know that this is a problem for many religiously committed women, and I am not sure how to solve it. My best suggestion is to do with the issue of God's gender what we do with the issue of God's anatomy, the references to God's eyes, ears, face, and so on. We use the traditional language and keep on reminding ourselves that it is meant metaphorically and not literally.

We heed Maimonides' warning that we can speak only negatively about God. We can deny what describes Him misleadingly; we cannot describe what He is. Yet there is one key moment in Jewish life when we seem to be making affirmations about God, talking about what God *is*, or at least affirming what He *does*. At the heart of any Jewish prayer service, Sabbath, festival, or weekday, is the prayer known as the *Amidah,* the prayer of the Eighteen Benedictions. It has eighteen benedictions (actually nineteen; one was added later) only in its weekday version; on Sabbaths, most of the paragraphs are omitted as not being in the spirit of the Sabbath. It is the weekday formulation I will be discussing. Even Jews who recite it regularly are largely not aware of the fact that it is one of the most comprehensive theological statements in all of Judaism, an inventory of the moments in our lives when we encounter God. (The text of the weekday Amidah appears at the end of this chapter.)

What do we affirm about God when we recite this liturgy each morning and evening?

—That the God to whom we pray is the God whom our ancestors discovered and worshipped, so that when we turn to God in prayer, we are defining ourselves as their descendants. Solomon Schechter, the founder of Conservative Judaism, once wrote that in contrast to Christianity's doctrine of "original sin," Judaism believed in "original virtue." We are born with the presumption of closeness to God because we are the great-grandchildren of Abraham, Isaac, and Jacob. Our Jewish identity is shaped less by our direct relationship to God, and more by our relationship to our parents and grandparents, and the generations of Jews who preceded them and passed a faith on to us. We turn to God because we are their descendants, and God cares about us because we are their descendants.

—That God grants immortality to the dead. Not only do we not know what goes on after this life ends, we could not understand what it would feel like to exist as a disembodied spirit even if someone could describe it to us. But we insist that death is not the end, that people live on in our hearts, in the difference they made to the world, and in the mind of God. It is through God's investing our lives with significance that we become immortal, and the prospect of dying becomes less fearful.

—That God is the source of holiness. To the objective, scientific mind, every day is the same, twenty-four hours long. But we know that days are different one from another. Some pass without a trace; others leave our lives permanently changed. One of the things that makes us human is our ability to sense that an anniversary, a birthday, a holiday is different from the days around it. Physically, one book is no different from another. We, in our humanity, can see some books as sacred. God is the source of our unique human ability to recognize the invisible qualities that make some objects, some buildings, some blocks of time sacred.

—That God helps us grow and change. When is God? When does God become real in our lives?

When something that used to be hard suddenly becomes something we can do (for children, there are few more inspiring discoveries). When we can look back and measure how much wiser and more understanding we have become over time. We identify God as the source of that growth.

—That God forgives. God's forgiveness is not so much a claim that God is no longer angry at us. It is a description of our coming to feel acceptable in His presence despite our mistakes, no longer condemned to carry the burden of past errors. We recognize that cleansing feeling as an encounter with God. The man who is so wrapped up in his work that he forgets his wedding anniversary needs to feel forgiven by his wife, not so that he can keep on repeating that mistake but precisely so that he can know that he doesn't have to continue being that kind of person. She doesn't see him as permanently, hopelessly forgetful, so he doesn't have to see himself that way either. And the man who is so involved with himself that he has shut his ears to the cries of the poor and has neglected the spiritual dimension of life needs to feel God's forgiveness as the first step in outgrowing that smallness of soul.

—That God heals the sick. Not that He heals every sick person or even that He chooses who will recover and who will remain ill, but that when we do recover from illness, the remarkable recuperative powers of our bodies and the skill and dedication of the doctor come from God. Again, God's power "is not the power to control, but the power to enable."

—That God causes the rain to fall, the crops to grow, and the resulting food to nourish us. The Israelites of old were farmers. They knew that no matter how hard they worked, the harvest depended on the heavens bringing rain and the earth working its miracle of transforming seeds, soil, and water into appetizing, nourishing food. We who live in a world of abundant packaged food in supermarkets are reminded in our prayers of that ultimate dependence.

—That God stands for justice, punishing the wicked and upholding the innocent. If some readers would be more comfortable with a prayer that spoke of God's "*forgiving* the wicked and upholding the innocent," I would offer the comment of the sages that "he who is kind to the cruel ends up being cruel to the kind." That is, when you do not hold a criminal responsible for his wrongdoing, not only do you diminish his humanity (being responsible for our behavior is what distinguishes human beings from animals), not only do you dilute the ability of the average person to count on justice when he feels wronged, but you run the risk that instead of being transformed by your act of forgiveness, he will merely be set free to victimize someone else. (I would emphasize here that the discussion is about justice, not vengeance, which is justice contaminated by the satisfaction of hurting somebody in the process.)

—That God has a special love for the Jewish people, the land of Israel, and the city of Jerusalem.
We have discussed earlier the issue of God's
choosing the Jewish people in love, that He feels
love and concern for all His creatures, human
and otherwise, but Israel is His firstborn (as He
refers to us in Exodus 4:22). The Jews were the
first community to know God and to make God
known in the world. Therefore He retains a special affection for them and has special hopes for
them, even as a human parent might feel for her
firstborn child. Let me add a word at this point
about Jerusalem, a city I lived in as a graduate
student, visit frequently, know and love. It is
holy to three great faiths and beloved by millions of religious people. But only Jews center
their prayers on it. We face Jerusalem when we
pray. We orient our synagogues to face it. The
traditional Jew mentions Jerusalem in his prayers
fifteen or twenty times *a day,* and still fasts on
Tisha B'Av, the anniversary of its destruction by
the Babylonians twenty-five centuries ago.

—That God will ultimately make the world the
kind of place He intends it to be (which is my
way of paraphrasing the anticipation of the Messiah). If Murphy's Law tells us that anything that
can go wrong will go wrong, the Jewish response to Murphy's Law is that anything that
should be one day *will* be—not always and not
immediately, but ultimately things will turn out
as they should. It is not so much a promise
("Don't worry, everything will be all right") as

it is a message of hope ("Don't give up; what your soul yearns to see is not impossible").

THE WEEKDAY AMIDAH PRAYER

(What follows is a contemporary rendering of the traditional weekday Amidah, by Rabbi Andre Ungar of Woodcliff Lake, New Jersey. It is reprinted from the *Siddur Sim Shalom* of the Rabbinical Assembly, edited by Rabbi Jules Harlow, *by permission of the Rabbinical Assembly. It is not a literal translation, but a faithful and religiously accurate rendition. I suggest that you read it, not as a script for your dialogue with God, but as a roadmap to all the ways in which God can become real in our lives.*)

1) Our ancestors worshiped You. Abraham and Sarah, Rebecca and Isaac, Jacob, Rachel and Leah stood in awe before You. We too reach for You, infinite, awesome, transcendent God, source of all being whose truth shines through our ancestors' lives. We, their distant descendants, draw strength from their lives and from Your redeeming love. Be our help and shield, as You were theirs. We praise You, God, Guardian of Abraham.

2) Your power sustains the universe. You breathe life into dead matter. With compassion, You care for those who live. Your limitless love lets life triumph over death, heals the sick,

upholds the exhausted, frees the enslaved, keeps faith even with the dead. Who is like you, God of splendor and power incomparable? You govern both life and death. Your presence brings our souls to blossom. We praise You, God who wrests life from death.

3) Sacred are You, sacred Your mystery. Seekers of holiness worship You all their lives. We praise You, God, ultimate sacred mystery.

4) The mind is Your gift, wisdom a spark from You. May we grow in knowledge, insight, and understanding. We praise You, God, gracious giver of awareness.

5) Help us to find our way to Your truth again, to obey You with trusting faith, to attain wholeness in Your presence. We praise You, God who is always ready to help us start anew.

6) Forgive our failures with a parent's love, overlook our shortcomings with regal generosity, for You are gentle and gracious. We praise You, God of mercy and forgiveness.

7) See our suffering, sustain us in our struggles, save us soon. We praise You, God, our people's hope of redemption.

8) Heal us, O God, and keep us in health. Help us, that we might help ourselves, praising You always. Send true healing for all our pains, for

You are the Source of healing and compassion. We praise You, God from whom all healing comes.

9) Bless this year for us with prosperity. May the wealth of the earth and the rhythms of the seasons yield us a good harvest in abundance. We praise You, God whose blessings are as certain as the seasons.

10) Let freedom resound like a mighty ram's horn. Let our spirits soar, sustained by Your promise. May the scattered Jewish people find wholeness and renewal. We praise You, God who brings home the lost Jew.

11) May our ancient sense of justice be renewed, our classic sources of wisdom recovered. May sorrow and sighing vanish from our midst. May Your tenderness and pity, justice and compassion govern our lives always. We praise You, God of kindness and justice.

12) May malice abate and ill will perish, may hatred cease and arrogance quickly wither in our lifetime. We praise You, God whose awesome power helps good to triumph over evil.

13) For the loving and the righteous, for the learned and the wise, for the stranger and for our own selves as well, may Your mercy

appear and Your justice be made manifest. May we be counted among the good, may we never regret having trusted in You. We praise You, God, strength of the just, root of our confidence.

14) Let Your love once more shine from Jerusalem. Let Your Presence abide there as in days of David. Let Zion rebuilt soon stand firm, the hub of Jewish hope forever. We praise You, God, builder of Jerusalem.

15) May our people flourish, all of them and soon. Help us to hold our heads high, celebrating Your deliverance and ours. Every day and all day long we yearn for Your deliverance. We praise You, God by whose will we survive and flourish.

16) When we cry out, hear us with compassion; take our prayers gently and lovingly. Listen to Your people when we reach toward You with love. Let us not turn away from You empty. We praise You, God who cherishes prayer.

17) Would that Your people at prayer gained delight in You. Would that we were aflame with the passionate piety of our ancestors' worship. Would that You found our worship acceptable and forever cherished Your peo-

ple. If only our eyes could see Your glory perennially renewed in Jerusalem! We praise You, God whose Presence forever radiates from Zion.

18) You are our God today as You were our ancestors' God through the ages; firm foundation of our lives, we are Yours in gratitude and love. Our lives are safe in Your hand, our souls entrusted to Your care. Our sense of wonder and our praise of Your miracles and kindnesses greet You daily at dawn, dusk and noon. O Gentle One, Your caring is endless; O Compassionate One, Your love is eternal. You are forever our hope. Let all the living confront You with thankfulness, delight and truth. Help us, O God; sustain us. We praise You, God whose touchstone is goodness. To pray to You is joy.

19) O God from whom all peace flows, grant serenity to Your Jewish people, with love and mercy, life and goodness for all. Consider us kindly, bless us with tranquility at all times and all seasons. We praise You, God whose blessing is peace.

6

What We Believe About People

*B*RITISH SOCCER fans are notorious for responding to their teams' victories and defeats violently. After one particularly disruptive outburst, when a mob reacted to the home team's losing by breaking windows, destroying property, looting, and assaulting innocent bystanders, one man tried to justify his comrades' behavior by saying, "What do you expect? They're only human."

In contrast, I remember being in San Francisco when it was hit by an earthquake. As darkness settled on a city without electricity to illuminate its streets or operate its traffic lights, people of all ages and races began to emerge from their homes with flashlights to direct traffic at intersections and help pedestrians cross safely.

What does it mean to be human? Does it mean being "only human," subject to irresistible urges and temptations? Or does it mean being a uniquely caring, compassionate creature? Alongside our discussion of what Judaism believes about God, we offer this summary of what Judaism believes about humanity.

Human beings are different from all other living creatures. That is not a scientific statement; it is a religious one. The biological differences (prehensile thumbs, greater capacity for language) are relatively trivial. It is only when we approach the areas where biology is silent and the voice of religion is heard, when we speak of the human being's capacity for goodness, for self-restraint, for abstract thought, that the uniqueness of the human being emerges.

The Bible conveys that difference in its very first chapter, when it describes God creating all other animals, fish, and birds by fiat, by decree ("And God said, 'Let there be . . .' and there was . . ."). But the first human beings are created by a special act of divine providence, formed by God's own hands, brought to life by an infusion of God's own breath. From a historical-biological point of view, I don't believe that is how it happened. As a way of capturing the uniqueness of the human being, I find it a true story.

This claim of uniqueness is challenged in some scientific quarters by people who see Man as just another animal, responding instinctively to stimuli in his environment in exactly the same way that other living creatures do. I entered college planning to major in psychology, only to discover in my freshman year that the psychology department was controlled by a school of thought known as experimentalism. In the introductory course, we spent one hour all year on Freud's theories, and three hours each week counting how many times a white rat pressed a bar. When I complained to the professor that there were aspects of human behavior that we could never understand by studying rats and those were the ones I was most interested in, he patiently explained to me that the whole point of the course was to disprove that. I switched my major to literature.

Perhaps the most extreme advocate of that instinctive point of view was the late B. F. Skinner, who taught that human beings never do anything on their own, even if they think they do. They simply process stimuli in their environment and respond blindly, instinctively, no differently than animals or even plants. We don't give charity because we are compassionate or generous. We do it because a certain situation, a certain appeal, creates a level of discomfort in us so that, in an act that has no more moral value than scratching an itch, we do something to make the discomfort go away. We don't vote for Candidate A because we have carefully considered what he stands for. We vote for him because he has convinced us that he represents security and his opponent represents danger. We are following the same instinct for self-preservation when we pull the lever in the voting booth that any animal shows when it seeks shelter from the rain or hides from a predator. Skinner once wrote, "A poet writes a poem just as a chicken lays an egg." (I wonder if he felt the same way about his books.)

Judaism rejects that point of view, and I believe it has human experience on its side. Lots of animals make noises to communicate, but only human beings pray, apologize, persuade, and write poems, novels, or symphonies. Most animals mate to reproduce, and a few species mate with a single partner for life. But only human beings love, rape, feel jealous, commit adultery, or celebrate wedding anniversaries. The soldier or stranger who risks his life to protect someone else may, in the eyes of the biologist, simply be acting to preserve the species, no different from the termite that dies fending off invaders of its colony. But the grieving of the soldier's family and the gratitude of the person saved have no analogue in the animal or insect world.

The uniqueness of the human being is captured in the phrase that we are "created in the image of God." We have a moral dimension. We can be good or bad, where animals can only be obedient or messy. When Charles Darwin shocked the conventions of the nineteenth century with his theory that human beings were related to animals and did not represent a special creation, someone asked him, "Is there anything unique about the human being?" Instead of talking about upright posture or brain cavity size, Darwin answered, "Man is the only animal that blushes." To recognize that we have done wrong, to recognize that more might have been expected of us than we delivered, is part of the uniqueness of the human being. No other creature can do that. Animals (and little children) can realize that they are about to be punished for something they did, but only mature human beings can judge themselves.

Human beings are responsible for their behavior. As I write this, the state of California is debating the propriety of putting a convicted murderer to death. There is no question that he committed the multiple murders for which he was convicted. The question raised by his lawyers was whether he was responsible for what he did. They claim that he was abused as a child, and therefore grew up with a soul so twisted that he became a murderer. I don't want to get into the pros and cons of capital punishment, and I certainly don't want to minimize the brutalizing impact of child abuse. But it seems to me that when a lawyer says, "My client should not be punished because he was not responsible for his actions," he is saying, in effect, "My client is less than fully human." One of the hallmarks of being human is taking responsibility for our actions. By the same token, when we act as our own defense lawyers by trying to excuse ourselves on the grounds that "I couldn't help myself; something made me do it," we forfeit part of our own humanity in the process.

In Jewish law, children and the mentally ill are excused from most religious obligations on the grounds that they are not responsible for their behavior. (When a child becomes Bar Mitzvah, he leaves that exempt status and joins the company of those adults whom we expect to behave morally.) The implication is that if you are a mentally competent adult, you *are* responsible for what you do. (Being angry, being neurotic, having had a less-than-perfect childhood do not excuse you from the obligations of the mentally competent.) "I'm only human" is no excuse; "I am human" is a challenge, not a justification.

When Judaism teaches that we are responsible for our actions, it is telling us that we are responsible for what we *do,* not what we think, dream, or fantasize about. When a woman comes to my office and tells me that she feels guilty, she feels like a bad person, because she dreamed of having an affair with her boss, I can absolve her of guilt by telling her that dreams don't count as long as she doesn't do anything to turn them into reality. When a man tells me that he is so angry with his neighbor that he fantasizes throwing a rock through the neighbor's picture window, I can tell him that angry thoughts are no sin, they are very normal, as long as he keeps his hands to himself. (I can also tell him that he would be a happier person by dissipating those angry thoughts rather than dwelling on them, but that is another subject.)

Salman Rushdie has been sentenced to death by Muslim extremists because a chapter in his novel The *Satanic Verses* offended Muslim sensibilities. A year or two earlier, the movie *The Last Temptation of Christ* was picketed by Christian fundamentalists because of a sequence portraying Jesus in an all-too-human light. What is fascinating about these cases is that in both the novel and the movie, the offending sections occurred in dreams. But to the fundamentalist mind, dreams are as real as deeds. Sins you commit in your imagination are as real, and as sinful, as deeds you actually perform. In 1976, presidential candidate Jimmy Carter admitted that he had "committed adultery in [his] heart" by noticing that women other than his wife were sexually attractive. He seemed to feel very guilty about it, though there is no evidence that he ever did anything wrong. Judaism could have told him that it is perfectly normal, perfectly human to notice attractive women and wonder what it would be like to sleep with them. It is also thoroughly human to resist that temptation.

The other implication of the Jewish teaching that we are responsible only for what we do is that we get no credit for those good impulses we believe in, intend to do, promise to do but never get around to acting on. Just as the sin we only fantasize about is no sin, the good deed we believe in but never do is no good deed. To believe that it is a good thing to feed the hungry and shelter the homeless, but not to do anything about it, does not qualify anyone as a good person.

Baseball umpires have a hard enough time calling balls and strikes, calling runners safe or out. But their job becomes impossible when they are asked to judge intentions: was the pitcher deliberately trying to hit the batter, or did the pitch just get away from him? Judaism recognizes the impossibility of our reading another person's mind by telling us that we are judged by our deeds, not our thoughts. That is why Jewish theology is so different from Christian theology. Very little of it is about the nature of God, issues of belief. Most of it is about the will of God, issues of behavior.

*   *   *

Judaism minimizes the distinction between body and soul. Many religious traditions in the East and West see the human being as consisting of a pure soul trapped in a corrupt material body. The soul tries to busy itself with prayer and contemplation, but the body keeps getting distracted by food and sex. The goal of religion, therefore, is to develop the soul and diminish the body, in anticipation of that glorious moment of deliverance when the soul will be liberated from its prison of corruptible flesh and soar free into the world of spirit.

Judaism rejects that duality. First, it does not see death as liberation from earthly bondage and a graduation to a better world. It sees death as tragedy. Death puts an end to a person's ability to sanctify the world. The death of a good person diminishes God's presence on earth. Second, Judaism does not see the material world, the world of food and sex and sleep and other bodily needs, as being less worthy than the realm of the spirit. Nothing created by God is vile or useless. Everything can be made holy or made base by the way in which it is used. The Talmud tells of one of the sages seeing workers cleaning and decorating a statue of the emperor and musing, "If that statue, which is an image of a flesh-and-blood king, is worthy of being cared for so carefully, how much more so my body, which is an image of the King of Kings. "

*　　*　　*

Human beings are not always good, but they are capable of goodness. A friend of mine who teaches economics shared with me a joke that economists tell on themselves: If you ask an economist, "Will the stock market go up or go down?," he will answer, "Yes, but not right away." Similarly, if you ask a rabbi, "Are people naturally good or naturally bad?," his answer will be "Yes, they are." Some people are good, some people are bad, and most people are both. Doing the right thing is within the reach of all human beings, and feels right when they do it, but it does not come naturally. There seems to be a kind of moral law of gravity holding us down, making it easier to lie in the short run than to tell the truth, easier to sleep late than to get up on time, easier to care for ourselves than to worry about others.

One would have to avert his eyes from too much reality—too much crime, violence, selfishness, and deceit—to claim that people are basically good. But one would have to ignore too much human courage and kindness to claim, as some religions do, that even the best of people is a sinner.

The classic Jewish teaching on the subject is that each of us possesses two conflicting tendencies, known in Hebrew as the *yetzer ha-ra,* the evil impulse, and the *yetzer ha-tov,* the good impulse. I have always been uncomfortable with the terminology of "evil impulse" or "impulse to do evil." For me, it raises the theological problem of why God would create something evil in His world. I like to think of the *yetzer ha-ra* as the impulse to selfishness, the concern with oneself alone, somewhat like Freud's construct of the id, a blind, amoral, self-serving instinct.

I once heard a Christian clergyman try to make sense of the doctrine of Original Sin, the notion that we are inevitably destined to be sinners because we are imperfect human beings. He said that if you look at an infant in its crib or a little child in a playpen, you think to yourself, "He looks so innocent, how can he be a sinner?" But, he said, put two babies in the crib or two children in the playpen and see how quickly they start fighting. There is no innocence there.

I was unconvinced by his argument. Aside from the question of whether little children are held morally accountable for what they do and can therefore be spoken of as sinning, I didn't see that claiming your need for space or your right to your own toys was a sinful act, any more than it would be sinful for me to see my home as my private domain, not open to the public.

Some people, I must admit, are evil—vicious criminals, mass murderers, tyrants like Hitler and Stalin—and I have trouble explaining that. It may be that, just as some people are born color-blind or lacking in certain other physical properties, others are born without a conscience. It may be that a vulnerable personality collided with an unfortunate childhood experience to produce a monster. But problematic as they are, the Hitlers and Charles Mansons are rare exceptions. Most people may be weak and undependable, but they are not evil. They may do wrong things, but they do not deserve to be condemned as sinners. For Judaism, sin is a deed, not a condition. The task of religion, as we see it, is to teach people to control their *yetzer ha-ra,* their selfish impulse, rather than strive to eradicate it (Gandhi taught that anyone who owns more clothing than he needs to wear or eats more food than he needs to live is stealing from his neighbor; Judaism considers that point of view unrealistic) or let themselves be controlled by it (like those perpetually unfulfilled people for whom no amount of money, of jewelry, of fancy clothes is ever enough).

Interestingly, some Jewish sources teach that we are born with the *yetzer ha-ra,* the selfish impulse, but the *yetzer ha-tov,* the impulse to do good, does not emerge in us until we reach the age of thirteen. Might we speculate that the best English equivalents of *yetzer ha-ra* and *yetzer ha-tov* might be "nature" and "human nature," the part of ourselves we share with animals and the part of us that is uniquely human? Nature tells us from the time that we are children to claim as much of the world's good as we can. So, obeying that natural instinct, we rush to get the free food at the buffet even though we have a full refrigerator at home. We resent the people who sneak into line ahead of us at the airport even though the plane will take off with all of us at the same time no matter how early or late we board. But human nature offers us the satisfaction of generosity rather than selfishness, of sharing rather than winning.

Only human beings can make mistakes, and only human beings can realize their mistakes. I use a computer when I write my books. My computer is wonderfully fast and accurate, and I am grateful for that, but it is also incredibly stupid. If I make a mistake and type something that doesn't make sense, if I hit the wrong key and give an inappropriate command, it does the wrong thing I tell it to. My mailman, on the other hand, cannot process information as rapidly or accurately as a computer, but he delivers mail to me even when my name is spelled wrong or the address is incorrect. Part of the uniqueness of a human being is that we can make mistakes (including mistakes much more serious than spelling a name wrong), and we can recognize our mistakes, regret them, learn from them, and correct them.

In Jewish thought, a sin is not an offense against God, an act of disobedience. A sin is a missed opportunity to act humanly. The verb *to sin* in Hebrew is also used in the sense of "missing the target." When God created us free to choose between good and bad, He also gave us the capacity to know when we had chosen wrongly. Remember Darwin's comment that human beings are the only creatures that blush. God gave us the power to repent, which means not only to regret what we did, but to change as a result of what we have come to understand. In Judaism, repentance is not complete until you come into the same situation and this time choose differently.

Where some theologies consider human beings to be doomed because we cannot be perfect, because we inevitably will do some things wrong, Jewish theology is impressed by the fact that while human beings err, they also can acknowledge their error, and can grow. "When I see the heavens, the work of Your hands, the moon and stars that You set in place, what is Man that You are mindful of him, the human being that You take note of him? Yet You have made him but little lower than the angels, and crowned him with honor and glory" (Psalm 8:3-6). There is a point in our congregational prayers when we say, "We recognize God's holiness on earth even as the angels do in Heaven, using the words the prophet Isaiah overheard the angels saying to praise God: Holy, holy, holy is the Lord of Hosts." As we say those words, we rise on tiptoe, as if trying to express in our body language as well as in words the notion that we are striving to rise above the level of human fallibility. We know that we are human, imperfect, earthbound, but we also long to be better than we are.

In fact, some of the sages consider human beings to be on a higher moral plane than even the angels. Angels never do anything wrong. Human beings do lots of things wrong, but have the capacity (which angels lack) to learn from their mistakes and to grow.

Our century has learned much, perhaps too much, about what human beings are capable of doing and being. We have seen their capacity for cruelty and for heroism. It has been the century of Adolf Hitler and of Anne Frank (and of Miep Gies, the Dutch woman who risked her own life to hide the Frank family). It has been the century of mass murders and of medical breakthroughs, of business fraud and of unprecedented charitable generosity. What have we learned about what it means to be human? Perhaps that the sages of the Talmud were right about our being born with conflicting impulses, so that doing good is always possible but never easy, that the satisfaction of being truly human is proportionate to the inertia and moral gravity that we have to overcome in the effort. Perhaps Victor Frankl, a psychiatrist and a survivor of Auschwitz, said it best in the last line of his memoir, *Man's Search for Meaning:*

"We have come to know man as he really is. Man is that being who invented the gas chambers of Auschwitz; however he is also that being who entered those gas chambers with *Shma Yisrael* on his lips."

7

When We Pray

---

*J*EWS PRAY differently than Christians do. In Judaism, not only are the words we say and the language in which we say them different; our understanding of what it means to pray is different.

Some of the problems we have with prayer today have to do with our not being sure what we believe about God. But most of them, I believe, result from our having grown up in a predominantly Christian society and having learned to think about prayer in Christian terms. If we think of praying at all, our image is either a desperate family in a hospital (movie cliché: The doctor comes out of the operating room looking grim and says to the priest who is sitting with the anxious family, "We've done everything we can, Father; it's up to you now") or else Dennis the Menace on his knees at bedtime, instructing God as to whom he wants blessed. We have learned to think of prayer as bribing God, pleading with God, or educating God.

A colleague of mine tells the story of the time

he officiated at the wedding of the daughter of a prominent family in his congregation. The wedding was to take place in the family's spacious and elegant backyard, weather permitting. If the weather was bad, the ceremony would be moved indoors, very much a second-best alternative. About an hour before the ceremony, dark clouds began to gather ominously. The concerned mother of the bride took a twenty-dollar bill, gave it to her husband, and said, "Here, put this in the *pushke* [charity box]." Forty minutes later, the rain had held off but was still threatening. The mother gave her husband another twenty dollars for the charity box. The ceremony went off without a single raindrop. You will never convince that woman that it wasn't her dollars to charity that controlled the weather, until the day someone she loves is seriously ill, and she will give a thousand dollars to charity for that person's recovery. Then if it doesn't work, she will wonder why God changed the rules on her.

In biblical times, Jews worshipped God with animal sacrifices. This custom was not unique to Israel; it was the mode of worship for that part of the world. It reflected the sense that, in order for a person to take worship seriously, it had to cost him something. And it was rooted in the understanding that the fundamental religious emotion when it came to worship was not pleading but gratitude. Prayer was not about what we wanted but did not have. It was about what we had received without having earned it. At harvest time and lambing time, people would bring the first fruits of the field and the firstborn of their flocks to thank God for what He had done for them. Only after that would they presume to ask for more of the same.

When Solomon's Temple was built in Jerusalem, it became the center of public worship. It was the only legitimate place where animal sacrifices could properly be offered. Thus, when the Babylonians destroyed the Temple and much of the population was exiled to Babylonia, Jews were deprived of their familiar form of public worship and had to invent a new one. They began to gather in small groups in what would become known as synagogues (from the Greek, meaning "place of assembly, place where people come together") and offer their spoken prayers to God. In the years before the destruction of the Temple, the groundwork for this important change had been prepared by the prophets, who urged the nation to transcend the formalism of Temple sacrifices and give God their hearts and not only their property, and by the psalmists, who created forms of personal, verbal prayer to express thanks, hope, anguish, and need in individual and collective terms. Since the Judaism we know today is the product of that postbiblical era, Jewish prayer today has come to mean the reciting of words at home or in the synagogue.

Several features make Jewish prayer unique. First, in a Conservative or Orthodox synagogue, the service will be recited largely in Hebrew. A Reform service will be about one-third Hebrew and two-thirds English. This not only makes it hard for strangers and visitors to follow; it is beyond the capacity of most of the worshippers themselves to understand what they are saying. It may strike many of us as strange to offer prayers we don't understand, since we are accustomed to thinking of prayer as sharing our concerns with God. (It would seem less strange to a Moslem, millions of whom know just enough Arabic to read the Koran as an act of piety, without understanding it.) But while we see worship as a way of communicating with God, we don't necessarily take that to mean telling God something He would not otherwise know. Much, even most, of Jewish prayer involves people reciting the same words together.

You may be familiar with the research that has been done in the last twenty years on the two sides of the brain. The left brain controls verbal, intellectual thinking while the right brain controls emotional, aesthetic functioning. That is why a person who has had a stroke on the left side of his brain will be able to think, feel, and recognize, but not be able to express his thoughts in words. I suspect that prayer in Judaism, though it uses words, is a right-brain phenomenon. Its purpose is more emotional than rational. Asking "What does a prayer mean?" is as irrelevant as asking "What does a sunset mean?" or "What does a flower mean?"

I once expressed this left brain-right brain theory in a lecture I was giving, and a young woman told me afterward, "Rabbi Kushner, I can prove that you are right. I am a speech therapist. I work with stroke patients. I have a seventy-nine-year-old man who suffered a left-hemisphere stroke. He can't talk, he can't tell you his name, but he can recite the entire Jewish morning service by heart."

Praying in Hebrew, reciting words that are familiar but untranslatable, helps reinforce this sense of prayer's being an emotional-aesthetic experience rather than a rational-intellectual one. A friend of mine suggests that the Hebrew words function as a kind of mantra. They provide our rational side with something to keep it busy so that the nonrational part of us, usually repressed and kept in check by custom and society, can take off and soar. It permits us to do something that doesn't make sense, to fly off in search of God, without our left brain's being embarrassed by it and making us feel self-conscious.

The other advantage of praying in Hebrew without understanding it is that it spares you from the temptation to argue with the prayer book. My aphorism is "Liturgy unites, theology divides." When a hundred Jews are chanting a prayer in Hebrew, they are welded into a single congregation. When, instead of chanting the Hebrew, they contemplate the English translation (usually offered on the facing page of the Hebrew prayer book), that unity is lost as every one of them begins to challenge and analyze what he has just been saying.

Worship in Judaism is not a final exam in theology, in which God examines what we know and affirm. It is a quest for a certain kind of emotional-spiritual experience. It is not "talking to God" so much as it is using words and music to come into the presence of God in the hope that we will be changed by doing so.

At the spiritual center of the High Holy Day service is a prayer, *Netaneh Tokef,* that raises serious theological problems for me. It describes God writing down in His book the fate of each of us for the coming year. Theologically, I find that image troubling, and I have to work hard to recast it into a message I can accept. But on Rosh Ha-Shanah morning, when a thousand people are chanting it in unison, letting the Hebrew words and traditional melody express their anxieties about the coming year, it is a powerful liturgical moment. That is why congregations get so upset when the cantor introduces a new melody for a familiar prayer. It is not the meaning of the words that matters to us; it is the emotional-aesthetic, right-brain experience we crave.

One of the other features of Jewish prayer is that it is based on a fixed liturgy. Praying means reciting the words printed in the prayer book, saying what one is "supposed" to say, rather than sharing oneself spontaneously. (There are brief moments for personal, unscripted reflection mixed in with the set liturgy.) I think there are two reasons for this practice. First, a fixed liturgy confronts us with thoughts and affirmations that might not occur to us if we relied on our own imaginations, and says them better than we could phrase them ourselves. The very first page of the Jewish prayer book prods me to express my gratitude for having awakened alive to the new day, for the fact that my mind works, my eyes work, my arms and legs work. I give thanks for having clothes to put on and things to look forward to that day. Would I remember to be grateful for all these things every morning, especially on cold, gloomy mornings when I had not slept well and my body was stiff and sore, if I didn't have the prayer book to structure my thoughts for me? Could I express either my gratitude or my dependence on God more eloquently than do the psalms I recite each morning?

And the second reason is that the purpose of prayer is not so much to enlighten God or to plead my case before Him, but to make me part of a worshipping community. (You will recognize a familiar theme here: Judaism as a collective enterprise rather than an individual one; religion wholesale rather than retail, if you will.) When it comes to congregational prayer, I am tempted to suggest that the congregating is at least as important as the prayers we offer. Praying with a congregation offers us the message that we are not alone in our hopes, our fears, our aspirations. It invites us to transcend our individual isolation and lose ourselves in the group, to experience the sense of being part of something greater than oneself. (In a way, it is a little bit like Erich Fromm's suggestion in his book *The Art of Loving,* that when we join with another person in genuine love, not just for the gratification of our own needs, we find the ultimate cure for loneliness.)

In a Jewish worship service, there will be a dialectic, a pull in opposite directions, between my praying as an individual and my losing myself in the group. For parts of the service, the congregation will chant in unison. For other moments, I will be left in individual contemplation. For me, the two most moving moments of congregational prayer have been those times when I thrilled to be part of a vast throng chanting together and other times when I found my mind wandering off to pursue some new thought provoked by a line of a prayer I had read hundreds of times before but suddenly saw as if for the first time as I contemplated it in silent reflection. I find I am more likely to have that personal experience in a congregational setting than when I am praying alone.

Another distinctive feature of Jewish prayer is the *minyan,* the required quorum of at least ten worshippers (in an Orthodox synagogue, ten male worshippers) required for the saying of certain prayers. One can pray at home; indeed, most of the daily and Sabbath liturgy can be recited by a person alone. But the *minyan* is rooted in the understanding that human beings are social animals, that our awareness is changed and heightened by the presence of other people. (You can see the game better at home on television, but you feel yourself a part of it with a crowd around you at the ballpark. And the movie you remember as being so hysterically funny isn't nearly as funny when you watch it alone at home on your VCR.) Our prayers are directed to God, not to the people around us, but their presence as fellow congregants helps us see ourselves at that moment as praying people.

Indeed, even the Jew who prays alone at home in the morning never really prays alone. He knows that other Jews are reciting the same words at the same hour, and he finds almost all of the prayers in his prayer book phrased in the plural: "Grant *us* . . . bless *us* . . . accept *our* thanks, for You have given *us*. . . ."

The most prominent of the prayers that can be recited only with a *minyan* present, that is, it must be a public prayer, not a private meditation, is the prayer known as the Mourners' Kaddish. It is recited daily by a recently bereaved person for a year after the death of a parent, and for thirty days or more after the death of another family member, affirming the worshipper's ongoing faith in God and in God's world even in the wake of a bereavement. At the end of the service, mourners are asked to stand and recite it. It is perhaps the best available proof of my claim that Jewish prayer is an emotional, right-brain process rather than an intellectual one, for it is not the meaning of the words of the Kaddish that comfort the mourner. Indeed, the same prayer with minor variations is used elsewhere in the service to mark the end of one section and the commencement of another. The Mourners' Kaddish is effective because it is the traditional

Jewish response to loss, and because it is recited publicly, in the presence of other mourners. It works as a public prayer because the mourner feels the support of the congregation around him and because he sees other mourners rising to offer the prayer and feels less singled out in his misfortune. The word *Kaddish* means "act of sanctifying" (a related word is used for religious martyrdom), and the mourner performs an act of sanctification by proclaiming publicly that his faith in God's world has survived bereavement. In Judaism, holiness, sanctification, always refers to the way people relate to each other, never to an act of withdrawing from a sinful world into a life of greater purity.

A traditional Jew prays every day, morning and evening. The weekday liturgy is relatively brief; the one for Sabbaths and festivals is considerably longer, reflecting the notion that on a Monday or Wednesday morning, we have to rush through our prayers as though we were double parked, while on Saturday we have all the time we need to sing God's praises. Indeed, non-Jews attending their first Sabbath service, perhaps for a Bar Mitzvah, are often surprised that the service can be three hours long. (That is why so many synagogues provide comfortable cushioned seats rather than wooden pews.)

The daily service is built around several fixed points:

1. blessings of gratitude;

2. the reciting of a number of biblical psalms, to get us in the mood for praying;

3. the affirmation of *Shema Yisrael,* "Hear, O Israel, the Lord our God, the Lord is One";

4. a prayer known as the *Amidah,* the prayer said while standing (which we discussed in chapter 5), sometimes called *Shemoneh Esreh,* the prayer of the eighteen (later nineteen) paragraphs. It is cast in the form in which petitions were brought before a king in ancient days: three paragraphs praising God for His greatness and past goodness, a dozen paragraphs articulating our needs (health, prosperity, forgiveness, the redemption of the Jewish people, world peace), and three concluding paragraphs thanking God for giving heed to our petition;

5. a few concluding prayers.

On Sabbaths and festivals, the service is expanded to include a lengthy period of Torah study. The *Shemoneh Esreh* is repeated twice, but altered to omit the requests and concerns of the weekday. Instead, prayers of thanks for the gift of the Sabbath or festival are offered.

What does it mean for a Jew to pray? In many European languages, the words *to pray* and *to beg* or *plead* are identical or closely related. (In German, *beten* means both "pray" and "beg." The English word *precarious,* meaning "uncertain, unstable," comes from a Latin root meaning "prayed for.") The Christian concept of prayer consists largely of bringing our needs and requests before God. We think in terms of praying *for* something. There is a verb in Hebrew meaning "to pray," whose original meaning is probably something like "to submit to judgment," but the more accurate Jewish term for worship is *l'varech,* "to bless." What does it mean for us to bless God? Isn't it God who blesses us? The etymology of the word is enlightening. Its original root meaning is "to bend the knee." In Hebrew, to pray is not to ask, but to bend the knee before God. Prayer is essentially reverence, not petition. Even the prayer of the eighteen paragraphs, in which we seem to be asking God to give us things (peace, health, etc.) is not so much asking as admitting dependence. There are things we crave desperately and cannot get by our own means, no matter how rich, pious, or clever we are. We depend on God's grace. In Judaism, a prayer is "answered" not when we get what we were asking for, but when we are granted a sense of God's nearness. The prayer of a sick person is "answered" not by having his disease disappear, but by his gaining the sense of God's nearness, the assurance that his illness is not a punishment from God and that God has not abandoned him. The prayer of a single woman is "answered" not by God's sending her a husband, but by God's granting her a sense of her worth in His eyes as a person, married or not.

The 73d Psalm is a masterpiece, one of the great spiritual works of all time, and should be a lot better known than it is. Its writer describes how he had become discouraged with the state of the world, because he saw a world where wicked people prospered and righteous people suffered. "My feet had almost stumbled, my steps had well nigh slipped, for I was envious of the arrogant, when I saw the prosperity of the wicked. . . . All in vain have I kept my heart clean and washed my hands in innocence. For all the day long I have been stricken." (Psalm 73:2-3, 13-14) The psalmist then goes on to describe the solution to his dilemma: "It seemed a wearisome task until I went into the sanctuary of God. . . . Thou didst hold my right hand, Thou didst guide me with Thy counsel" (Psalm 73:16–17, 23–24). God "answers" his questions about the world's injustice not by explaining the suffering of the righteous or the prosperity of the wicked, but by granting him a sense of being in God's presence, and letting him realize that that is worth more than wealth and fame.

In the spirit of the 73d Psalm, Jewish prayer is not a matter of informing God as to what we believe and what we need, but of seeking His presence and being transformed by it. We don't ask God to change the world to make it easier for us. We ask Him only to assure us that He will be with us as we try to do something hard.

To this point, we have been using the words *prayer* and *worship* as if they were interchangeable. But there is a distinction between them. *Worship* refers to all of our efforts to come in contact with God. *Prayer* is the verbal form of worship, relating to God through spoken and sung words. For Jews, there are at least two other forms of worship that figure largely in our spiritual lives, and while not entirely unique to Judaism, they do reflect something of the Jewish soul.

Jews worship God through study. The central moments of a Sabbath morning service are dedicated to reading aloud not merely a brief passage from the Bible but several chapters of the Torah, so that in the course of the year, the entire Five Books of Moses will have been studied aloud. In the autumn, on Simchat Torah after the High Holy Days, we begin "In the beginning," with the Creation story, and week by week, chapter by chapter, omitting nothing (who are we to pass judgment on God's word, deciding that the story of Joseph and his brothers is edifying but the laws about leprosy and menstrual flow are not?), we come to the end of Deuteronomy just as we are running out of year and preparing for the Holy Day season again. At that point, we are ready to start all over again, finding new insights in the Torah, not because it has changed but because we have.

Why this emphasis on study? One of my seminary professors used to say, "When I pray, I speak to God. When I study Torah, I keep quiet and let God speak to me." If worship is the effort to connect with God, Judaism affirms that we don't have to do all the work ourselves. God is prepared to meet us halfway. By immersing ourselves in Torah, we transport ourselves back to Sinai, to the presence of God. Some people have used fasting, drugs, or forms of self-hypnosis to summon up the presence of God. We have never had to resort to those measures. Like the wife whose husband is away on a business trip and who conquers her loneliness by rereading his letters, we turn to the Torah and feel God's presence.

The most famous prayer in all of Judaism, *Shema Yisrael* ("Hear, O Israel, the Lord our God, the Lord is One") is technically not a prayer at all. That is, it is addressed to the Jewish people, not to God. It is a page out of the Torah (Deuteronomy 6) that says some important things about God and His Torah, and urges us to cherish the Torah day and night. By setting that page of Torah into the morning and evening liturgy, we enable people who might not have the time to study to have at least this twice-a-day contact with the life-sustaining power of the Torah.

A second reason for this unique emphasis on study is the Jewish perception that what is uniquely human about a person is his mind and his conscience. Our physical self is the part of us that we share with the animals. Our mind and conscience are the dimension we share with God. When we exercise our minds and consciences by studying God's word on how a person should live, when we occupy our thoughts with questions of how to carry out God's will rather than with matters of finance, fashion, or sports, we feel that we are developing our uniquely human aspect.

And finally, a Jew worships God and comes into God's presence by performing a *mitzvah,* a religious obligation, and as we do so, reciting the blessing praising God for having shown us the way to bring holiness into our lives through the *mitzvah.*

Martin Buber once defined theology as talking about God and religion as experiencing God.

He went on to say that the difference between them is the difference between reading a menu and having dinner. Theology can be enlightening, it can lead the way to nourishment, but it is not in itself nourishing. When we speak about God abstractly as the One who summons us to righteousness or as the One who causes the earth to grow food, that is theology. When we speak *to* God, saying, "Thank You for bringing holiness into my life by commanding me to do this," that is religion.

It is an embarrassing truth that fewer Jews attend services than do Catholics or Protestants. Every Gallup poll that asks, "How often do you attend a church or synagogue?" finds 50–60 percent of all Christians attending weekly or at least once a month, and only about 20 percent of Jews. Why the discrepancy? The pessimist in me says it is because our services are too long, our sermons aren't good enough, we have failed to educate people about the value of congregational prayer. The optimist in me says that it is because we have succeeded in educating Jews that you don't have to go to synagogue to worship God. When we study and reflect on how to be a good person, when we sanctify the most ordinary of moments by doing something because we feel commanded to do it, we are worshipping God at that moment.

8

Personal Milestones

---

*T*HE CEREMONIES and rituals with which Jews respond to the major moments of a person's life—birth, marriage, maturity, death—do not in themselves bring about a change. They celebrate or respond to the change that has taken place and guide us to see the deeper meaning, the divine presence hidden in the event. The ceremonies of welcoming a newborn Jewish baby do not make the baby Jewish; the child of a Jewish mother is Jewish from birth. Even a wedding ceremony does not join two people in marriage so much as it recognizes and celebrates the significance of their having linked their lives to each other.

And these rituals do something else as well. They give us a way of coming together with other people, to amplify our response to what is happening to us. There are few sadder things in life than to have something to celebrate or grieve for, and to have no one to share those feelings with.

In fact, the word *synagogue* means "place of coming together," emphasizing its congregating function more than its dimension of sanctity.

The architecture and interior design of a building, any building, tell a lot about what the building is for: Is it meant for large, anonymous crowds or small, intimate gatherings? Is it well lit so that things are seen clearly, or dimly lit to stimulate a sense of mystery? Do its furnishings imply a long stay (comfortable theater seats) or a short one (hard chairs in fast-food restaurants)?

What can we know about a synagogue just by walking in and looking around? First, if it is properly designed, our eye will immediately be drawn to the Ark, the curtained chamber at the center of the front wall, where the Torah scrolls are kept. It is the presence of the Torah scrolls that makes the room a synagogue, a holy place. The scrolls are the text of the Torah, the first five books of the Bible, hand-written on parchment and scrupulously checked to make sure that they are error-free and correctly copied. (In a Catholic church, your eye will be drawn to the altar; in a Protestant church, to the pulpit from which the word is preached. We use architecture to make a statement about what is important, where the building's spiritual center of gravity is located.) The Ark will typically be located on the eastern wall of the sanctuary, and seats will be arranged facing it, so that worshippers as they pray will be facing toward Jerusalem, site of Solomon's original Temple.

I happen to believe that most modern synagogues are built wrong. They invite you to sit back, typically into a cushioned seat, and watch a performance of professionals on a raised platform. Such a design encourages passivity, the feeling of being an audience, sitting, watching, and evaluating. I would prefer seeing the architecture encourage participation rather than passivity. And in fact, centuries ago, synagogues were built in the round, or seats were set in a horseshoe shape, with the pulpit in the middle, so that a Jew at prayer, when he looked up, saw other Jews at prayer rather than seeing clergy conducting the service.

For most of Jewish history, services were not conducted by professional clergy, but by knowledgeable laymen. (At weekday services and in many Orthodox synagogues, that is still the case today.) In biblical times, priests who attained their office by heredity (they were born to a father who was a priest, a Kohen, a descendant of Moses' brother Aaron) officiated at the sacrificial services at the Temple. After the Temple was destroyed, Jews would gather in homes to pray and study the Torah. The people most admired in the community were those who had studied the most and were best qualified to interpret the laws of the Torah for the community. They had no function at services, but were approached to judge legal disputes or to answer complicated religious questions. People who had mastered the study of Torah were honored with the title *rabbi,* meaning "teacher, master."

In more recent times, being a rabbi became a full-time profession, because there was more material to master and more questions to answer as we became less well informed about our tradition. And in American synagogues, the rabbi tended to take on the status and role of the Christian clergyman, becoming more of a pastor, officiating at services, visiting the sick, and counseling the troubled, rather than being a scholar and repository of knowledge.

The role of the cantor goes back further into Jewish tradition, but it too has been professionalized in recent years. The only requirements for leading a congregation in worship were that the leader be Jewish and know the prayers. (In Orthodox congregations, the leader would have to be a male, since by Orthodox law, women are excused from the obligation to pray at set times—they presumably have families to care for—and the leader of the service should be fulfilling his own prayer obligation while leading others to fulfill theirs. Liberal congregations hold that it makes no sense to excuse *all* women from prayer because *some* have family commitments.) In olden days, before there were fixed liturgies and printed prayer books, a service leader would be more valued if he knew the order of prayer by heart and could improvise eloquently on it (rather like a jazz soloist embellishing but ultimately returning to a theme). When prayers were set in type, a prayer leader would be chosen for his voice. When I first began attending services at a prominent Brooklyn synagogue in the 1940s, the cantor was Richard Tucker, who would go on to win international fame as an opera star. Today the chief requirement for a professional cantor is not that he possess an outstanding operatic voice, but that he or she (some of the best young cantors are women) have the sort of voice and style that will move people unaccustomed to praying to join in the service.

One other feature of synagogue architecture worthy of note is the light (a candle or electric bulb) hanging in front of the Ark. This is the Eternal Light, placed there in fulfillment of the charge in Exodus 27:20–21 to keep a light burning in the Tent of Meeting at all times, and symbolizing the invisible but eternal presence of God in a room where Torah scrolls are kept and people gather to worship.

In a traditional (Orthodox or Conservative) synagogue, men keep their heads covered with a small cloth skullcap (called a *yarmulke* in Yiddish or *kippah* in modern Hebrew). The origins of this custom are unclear. My own guess is that in the ancient Near East, the definition of being "dressed up" for a serious occasion included having your head covered. Going bareheaded was inappropriately informal, like showing up for a formal dinner or job interview today without a coat and tie. Because coming into God's presence was a serious matter, the Jewish man would keep his head covered. Indeed, many traditional Jews wear a *kippah* at all times, as a way of reminding themselves that, wherever they are and whatever they are doing, they are in God's presence.

Male worshippers in Orthodox or Conservative synagogues also wear a *tallit,* a large fringed prayer shawl at daytime services, though not at evening prayers. This is in fulfillment of the biblical passage (Numbers 15:37-41) commanding us to wear fringes on the corners of our garment to remind us of all the big and little ways in which we are commanded to serve God, a little like tying a string around one's finger to remind you that you were supposed to remember something. In some Conservative synagogues, some women may also choose to wear the *tallit,* to express the sense that they too are commanded to serve God in big and little ways.

The major celebration of a transitional moment in a person's life that takes place in the synagogue is the Bar Mitzvah ceremony. In Jewish life, a child is under the authority of his or her parents until the age of thirteen. The assumption is that the child will obey the parents or that the parents will be able to control their child. Adolescent and grown children, however, are responsible for their own behavior. (Notice how the word *responsible* keeps creeping into so many of our explanations.) The Bar/Bat Mitzvah ceremony celebrates the young person's coming of age, "graduating" from childhood to adult status.

After thirty years as a congregational rabbi, and after seeing both of our children go through the ceremony (promising myself I would not be caught up in it the way all those other parents were, and then promptly breaking that promise), I still don't understand the emotional hold that the Bar Mitzvah ceremony has on Jewish families. Why do parents who are otherwise uncommitted to Jewish learning and synagogue life drive their children to Religious School three times a week for five years? Why do families take out bank loans to pay for an elaborate birthday party for a bewildered thirteen-year-old? Why is it that if we advertise that "Rabbi Kushner will lecture on the question of whether God exists," a dozen curious people will turn out, but if we say, "Rabbi Kushner will discuss a proposal to change Bar Mitzvah requirements," it's standing room only? Partly, I think, a Bar Mitzvah ceremony is like any "graduation" event. It provides parents with the badly needed reassurance that they have successfully and responsibly brought their child to a major turning point in his or her life. But clearly, more than that is involved. Seeing a son or daughter at the Torah affirming his or her Jewish identity assures the parent of spiritual immortality. It means that an important part of you will live on for another generation.

After all, if the child is thirteen, how old are the parents likely to be? Probably in their mid-to-late thirties for the first child, perhaps mid-forties by the time the youngest turns thirteen. They are at an age when issues of mortality and vicarious immortality are beginning to mean more to them. To have their son or daughter, on the threshold of independence, proclaim publicly, "I will continue to carry on the family identity. No matter what struggles I may go through as an adolescent, I will always be your child, your parents' grandchild, the next link in the chain of generations," is something the parents deeply need to hear, whether they realize it or not.

If you have got the impression from the above paragraph that a Bar/Bat Mitzvah ceremony is more important to parents than to their thirteen-year-old children, you are correct psychologically even if not according to the literal meaning of Jewish law. When we would ask our thirteen-year-old Bar Mitzvah candidates, "Why are you doing this? What does it mean to you?," virtually none of them spoke of Jewish identity. They all said, "To please my parents, to make them proud of me," or "I'm doing it because it's important to my parents." Of course, in doing something Jewish that is important to their parents, they are upholding an important principle of Judaism. But it is equally important for the child on the brink of adolescence and the challenge of becoming his own person to know that his parents are proud of him. For the boy to know that his father approves of his entering manhood and independence, for the girl to know that her mother is not jealous of her emerging femininity, is truly an important gift.

I would constantly remind my congregants that a Bar Mitzvah is not a party, nor is it a ceremony. Least of all is it a verb, as in "Rabbi, you may not remember it, but you bar mitzvahed our son ten years ago." A Bar Mitzvah is a thirteen-year-old Jewish boy. By now, you recognize the word *mitzvah,* the sacred deed. *Bar* is the Hebrew-Aramaic word for son, *Bat* is the Hebrew for daughter. You may have seen the term *Bar Mitzvah* translated as "son of the commandment," which may have puzzled you since commandments generally do not have children. A more intelligible rendering of the phrase would be "member of the *mitzvah* system," that is, a person both qualified and expected to perform the *mitzvah* in a way that he or she was too young to do before. There are only two requirements for becoming Bar Mitzvah: You have to be Jewish and you have to have reached the age of thirteen. No ceremony, no rabbinic benediction is required. As in all Jewish life-cycle events, the ceremony does not effect the change; it celebrates it.

But although a Jewish adolescent could technically become Bar/Bat Mitzvah simply by waking up on his or her thirteenth birthday, the transition from child to adult is deemed so important that months of study and planning go into the event. The youngster is asked to demonstrate that he or she has acquired the skills necessary for living a Jewish life—a knowledge of the laws, an ability to read from the Torah and conduct the service. (The late Joseph Campbell once said that if societies do not fashion ordeals for adolescents to go through to prove that they are worthy of being taken seriously as adults, they will create them for themselves, inventing all sorts of dangerous tests of their manhood.) The Bar/Bat Mitzvah ceremony contains elements of the adolescent ordeal, the challenge to prove yourself worthy of being an adult. I suspect that the bizarre story in Genesis 22, about Abraham being commanded to kill his son Isaac on the altar as a sacrifice, contains within it the memory of some sort of adolescent ordeal that Isaac had to survive to gain the status of a committed adult.

The idea behind Bar Mitzvah is an old one, drawing a legal line between being a child of whom little was demanded except obedience and being a responsible adult. By the second or third century, age thirteen was seen as the legal age of responsibility. But the ceremony of celebrating a child's reaching that milestone, as an ordeal of entry into adult status, was a late medieval invention. Before that, young Jews began to assume adult responsibilities at age thirteen, but never had a service or party to mark that change. There are probably elderly Jews living today whose Bar Mitzvah ceremony consisted of being called to read from the Torah on their thirteenth birthday and some cake and whiskey for the congregants afterward. They may be understandably bewildered by the extravagances of their grandchildren today.

The ceremony of welcoming the Bar Mitzvah to his new status takes place in the context of a Sabbath morning service. In a large congregation where the number of youngsters turning thirteen in a given year exceeds the number of Saturdays available, two or more families may be celebrating at the same Sabbath service. In some synagogues, the youngster may lead the entire service.

In others, his participation may be fairly brief. But typically, the crucial moment will come during the reading of the Torah. The Bar Mitzvah's parents, and perhaps other relatives, will be among the congregants honored by being called to the Torah to recite the blessings over the reading, and the Bar Mitzvah himself will usually be given the longest and most challenging portion to read, as a way of demonstrating beyond doubt his fitness to be welcomed as a Jewish adult.

Typically, a festive meal will follow the service. It may range from a luncheon with poignant remarks by a grandparent to a Saturday night black-tie gala that gives new meaning to the word excess. (In recent years, there has been a welcome and growing movement for the celebrant family to contribute 3 percent of the cost of a wedding or Bar Mitzvah celebration to a fund to feed the hungry, just as the Torah calls on us to include the poor and the needy in our celebrations, and to donate the flowers to a local hospital or nursing home. It is also a custom in many synagogues to ask the Bar Mitzvah to designate a charity to which he will send a percentage of his monetary gifts, as a sign that he has accepted this form of adult responsibility.)

The Hebrew word for a wedding ceremony is *kiddushin,* an act of sanctifying. The marriage of a man and a woman is not merely a legal transaction or the legitimation of sexual intimacy. It is an acknowledgment by the couple of the intervention of God in their lives. When animals mate and reproduce, that is only biology. When human beings fall in love and marry, when they dare to put their happiness into another's keeping and make themselves vulnerable thereby, when they experience the joy of commitment and closeness, we believe that God is at work.

In a Jewish wedding ceremony, bride and groom stand under a canopy, whether of cloth or of flowers, symbolizing the community's recognizing them as a family. Traditionally, a young man and a young woman would not be permitted to be alone together under one roof unless they were married.

Bride and groom sip twice from a cup of wine, once at the beginning of the ceremony, just before the formula of betrothal, and again at the conclusion. In the language of Jewish symbolism, wine characterizes the moment as being both sacred and joyous. The groom presents a ring to the bride in the sight of witnesses and says, "Behold, thou art consecrated unto me by this ring as my wife, according to the law of Moses and the Jewish people." (In a non-Orthodox ceremony, the bride reciprocally presents a ring to the groom.) A portion of the *ketubah,* the marriage contract, is read, in which they promise to support each other in love and faithfulness. Seven blessings are chanted, praising God for giving us the capacity to love and be faithful to another person, and for giving us such a gratifying way to perpetuate the species, and asking His blessings on the couple and the new home they have founded. At the end, in the most unique and dramatic moment of a Jewish wedding, the groom steps on a glass and breaks it.

The explanations of the breaking of the glass are many, from the suggestion that loud noises scare away demons (as on New Year's Eve) to the wish that the marriage last until the pieces come together again. In the ancient Near East, contracts were often sealed by writing on a clay tablet a series of curses that would befall the person who violated the terms of the contract. The tablet was then broken. All of these fanciful interpretations aside, the origin of the custom is recorded in the Talmud. At one wedding feast, we are told, the merriment of the guests threatened to get out of hand. The host took an expensive plate and broke it, just to sober people up and cause them to reflect on the fragility of life and happiness. The breaking of the glass at a wedding, then, would represent the typical Jewish reminder that, even at the moment of our greatest personal joy, we cannot let ourselves forget the many people who have less reason to rejoice than we do. In Judaism, we relate this awareness to the destruction of the Temple, the enduring symbol of the world's evil trying to extinguish the flame of holiness. We are still part of a human race darkened by so much pain and sorrow. We will appreciate the joy of the moment more when we realize how fragile it is.

What doesn't happen at a Jewish wedding, that you might anticipate from other marriage ceremonies you have attended? One element that is missing is the question of "who gives this woman away?" Jewish brides are delighted to learn that the ceremony doesn't see them as being transferred from the custody of one adult male to the custody of another. It sees the bride as a responsible adult making a commitment of her own life. In fact, technically, the rabbi doesn't marry the couple. He serves as a witness for the state and for the Jewish community to the act of their marrying each other.

And you will rarely hear "Here Comes the Bride" played at a Jewish wedding. The melody comes from the opera *Lohengrin,* whose composer, Richard Wagner, was a rabid antisemite, making it inappropriate for his music to be used in a Jewish religious ceremony.

From time to time, I am asked to officiate at a wedding where one of the participants is Jewish and the other is not. I have to explain to the couple that I am not able to. It's not that I don't wish them happiness; I certainly do. But I take the Jewish wedding ceremony seriously, and its words and rituals do not apply to non-Jews (even as a Catholic priest can sincerely admire the piety of devout Jews or Muslims, but cannot administer communion to them). I urge such couples to find a spiritually inclined justice of the peace who will perform a nondenominational service for them in which the presence of God will be acknowledged, but nobody will be asked to recite words or perform acts in which he or she does not believe.

Jewish weddings are recognizably similar to non-Jewish wedding ceremonies, and our non-Jewish neighbors have religious traditions—confirmation, first communion—analogous to the Bar Mitzvah, to celebrate their children's coming of age religiously. But I know of nothing in any religious tradition to compare to a *bris*, the ritual circumcision of a newborn Jewish boy.

Circumcision involves the surgical removal of the foreskin from the male sex organ. In a world where most religious rituals consist of words and gestures, a world in which explicit references to sexual organs, let alone involvement of sexual organs in religious ritual, is rare, circumcision is certainly unique. It is an ancient ceremony, one that retains its power to move us even as it makes us anxious and uncomfortable. The circumcision ceremony usually takes place in the home a week after the birth of a son, on the eighth day of the child's life as commanded in Genesis 17:12, unless medical complications necessitate a postponement. Although it is the father's responsibility to circumcise his newborn son, the ritual is virtually always performed by a specialist known as a *mohel,* who is an expert in the procedure. He may or may not be a physician, but he should be a pious and learned person who is familiar with the ritual and religious aspects of a *bris* as well as the surgical ones. Often, people will feel squeamish, avert their eyes, even leave the room during the brief ceremony, returning for the festive meal (is there ever a Jewish gathering without one?) a few moments later. Technically, a *bris* ceremony is not required to make the child Jewish (unlike, say, an infant baptism). The exception is the case where the child's mother is not Jewish and the circumcision is for purposes of converting the infant to Judaism. Yet, over the centuries, Jews have risked humiliation and danger to fulfill this commandment.

What is this rite, so different from anything else we do in our Judeo-Christian society? Like other Jewish rites, it does not change things; it celebrates them. In this case, what is being celebrated is the continuity of Jewish identity, passed on from father to son. At the *bris*, the child is given his religious name. Typically he will be named after a deceased relative, to give that relative a measure of immortality, to "make the name live on" and to emphasize that the newborn child is the latest link in a long chain. Presumably the foreskin is designated to be removed from the generative organ to symbolize the fact that Jewish identity is passed on by birth, from father to son, from generation to generation.

In the ancient Near East, many societies circumcised their male children. In the story of Saul and David in First Samuel, the Philistines, a Greek people rather than a Semitic tribe, were considered unusual and referred to as "the uncircumcised" because they did not practice that custom. But in that era, boys were circumcised when they became adolescents, as a preparation for being sexually active and as an ordeal of entry into the adult community. (And you thought studying for a Bar Mitzvah ceremony was hard!) Ancient Judaism removed the sexual dimension from the ritual by moving it back to infancy.

The complete name of the ritual is *bris* (or *brith*) *milah,* with the second word meaning "circumcision" and the first word (as you may remember from an earlier chapter) meaning "covenant." The circumcision ceremony identifies the Jewish child as a member of the Covenant with God by virtue of his birth as a Jew into a Jewish family.

Obviously the week-old infant is in no position to understand what is happening to him. But as he grows older and learns about it, and as he one day arranges for a similar ceremony for his own son, he comes to comprehend the twofold meaning of the *bris*: A Jew is born into the Covenant with God whether he wants to be or not, and this Covenant involves pain and sacrifice as well as honor and sanctity. He may grow up to be a good Jew or a bad Jew (however that is defined). But he cannot ignore his Jewish identity. Like his parents, like his physical traits and the century and country of his birth, it is one of the facts of his life. As in the Book of Jonah, as in the Book of Ezekiel, God pursues us even when we would rather not deal with Him. The Covenant can be violated; it cannot be escaped. It is part of who you are, branded into your flesh at birth.

The opening words of the *bris* ceremony invoke the presence of Elijah the prophet. Two reasons are traditionally given for this. One, which we will recognize from the Passover Seder, sees Elijah as the forerunner of the Messiah, the one who will come and tell us that the

Messianic Age is imminent. Every time a Jewish child is born, the parents and the community speculate, "Will he be the one? Will this child grow up to make the world a different, better place, a place more fit for God?" We anticipate Elijah's arrival at the welcoming of any Jewish child into the Covenant.

The second reason is based on a passage in the Book of Kings (I Kings 19:14), where Elijah complains to God about the faithlessness of the Israelites, saying, "They have forsaken Your covenant." God is offended by Elijah's dismissal of an entire people, and to teach him a lesson, sentences him to attend every ceremony where a Jewish family welcomes a newborn son into the Covenant, as if to say to him, "How can you speak that way about My people? Look at them. They may not be totally observant in many matters, but they have not forsaken My Covenant."

Old Jewish joke: What is the technical term for a Jewish child who does not have a *bris*? Answer: She is called a girl. It may have occurred to the astute reader that this important ceremony can be performed for only 50 percent of Jewish children. How is the Jewish identity of a newborn daughter celebrated?

One of the exciting developments of the twentieth century has been the slow but steady recognition of women as equally valid partners in the public celebration of Judaism. The ceremony of Bat Mitzvah evolved to become the equivalent of a boy's Bar Mitzvah celebration. (As of this writing, the first person ever to celebrate becoming Bat Mitzvah is still alive.) And ways of welcoming a Jewish daughter were invented. The most common is the naming of a child at a Sabbath morning Torah reading. The parents are called to the Torah, offer a prayer of thanksgiving, and confer a religious name on their daughter. Alternately, a home ceremony paralleling the *bris* in its stress of identity, naming, and gratitude to God for the new life can be held.

In the interests of completeness, let me mention briefly a ceremony that was extremely rare thirty years ago and is now performed thousands of times annually—the ceremony of converting a gentile to Judaism. Once upon a time, Jews were active missionaries. In a world where we were the only adherents of monotheism, the faith in One God, we saw it as our duty to wean pagans from idol worship to the worship of God. For much of the last fifteen centuries, a combination of circumstances—that Christian and Muslim laws made it illegal and that most gentiles were now not pagans but Bible-affirming monotheists—limited the scope of Jewish conversionary activity. But in the freedom of the modern world, where people can choose where they want to live, what work they will do, and what religion, if any, they will practice, doors have suddenly opened in the walls that separated one religion from another. Some non-Jews became Jews because their study of the Bible or their response to Jewish efforts to improve the world convinced them that Judaism offered them the spiritual home they were searching for. (The mystics speak of "Jewish souls mistakenly born into gentile bodies.") Most non-Jews who become Jews do so for reasons of marriage to a Jewish man or woman, and out of the desire to share a single religion in their home rather than have it be religiously divided.

How do you become Jewish? You study for the better part of a year. You affirm that you understand that you are joining a community, not just affirming a theology (like Ruth in the Bible, who said, "Your people will be my people," and only afterward added, "and your God my God"). You are interviewed by a panel of three rabbis constituting a religious court, who will do their best to discourage you by pointing out the religious and social hardships of being Jewish. And finally a male candidate is circumcised if he was not as a child, and the candidate, male or female, is immersed in a bathing pool known as a *mikvah*. In biblical times, Jews would immerse themselves for purposes of ritual cleansing if they had become ritually impure. But the immersion of the convert is not for purposes of cleansing him or her of the "impurity" of being a gentile. We are not saying, "You used to be dirty and now you will be clean." The immersion is a rebirth ceremony. As you were first born out of water into the air, so do you now reenter the water and emerge as a new person to a new identity. The convert is then given a new name (which he or she gets to choose) for use on future religious occasions.

We have saved for last our consideration of the ways in which Judaism teaches its adherents to respond to death and bereavement. We have, alas, had all too much experience in burying our dead and drying the tears of the bereaved, and we have learned much about the human soul in the process. Comforting the grieving in time of loss may be one of the things Judaism does best. I have seen it work its magic hundreds of times on people who thought religion could do nothing for them in their anguish.

When a person dies, the first rule of Jewish mourning is to arrange for a funeral as soon as possible, the next day if feasible. There are no visiting hours before the funeral, no prefuneral wake, and almost never any viewing of the body. Our philosophy of grieving holds that the mourner is too numb, in a state of suspended animation, and can begin the work of grieving and healing only at and after the funeral service. (A quirk of Jewish law states that, should the newly bereaved person attend synagogue between the death and the burial, he is not counted toward the *minyan,* the quorum required for public prayer, on the theory that he may be there physically, but emotionally he is not really present. The same, by the way, holds true for a bridegroom the morning after his wedding.)

On the day of the funeral (which can never take place on a Sabbath or festival), the mourner tears a part of his or her clothing (or a ribbon pinned to the clothing), an ancient symbol of grief. The service may take place in a synagogue (especially if the deceased was known for his or her piety), or in a special chapel maintained by the funeral director. On rare occasions (I discourage it except when the deceased was very elderly and outlived most of her friends and relatives), the service may take place at the graveside. It consists of a few psalms, a eulogy paying tribute to the deceased and offering comfort to the mourners, and a memorial prayer.

One of the unique Jewish responses to bereavement is the recitation of the Mourners' Kaddish, an ancient prayer praising God for the world He has given us. The words of the Kaddish would seem to have the mourner saying, "Even at a time and place like this, I am grateful for the world and all the good things with which my life was blessed." But I suspect that the Jewish mourner reciting the Kaddish and being comforted by it is responding not to the words but to the music. Saying Kaddish is not a theological pronouncement. It is the traditional Jewish way of responding religiously to a death. The prayer says more than the words say. The prayer says, "At a moment like this, contemplating my mortality and that of everyone I know, I know that I am a Jew and I reach out to the Jewish tradition to channel God's healing love into my life." I have lost three family members over the years, both my parents and a fourteen-year-old son. On each occasion, I discovered (and rediscovered) that the system works. In ways that transcend rational understanding, I was comforted by going to the synagogue each morning and reciting the Mourners' Kaddish. I was comforted by the knowledge that I was doing what Jews have always done over the centuries. And I was comforted by the presence of other worshippers, half of them mourners like myself, trying to come to terms with the outrage of death and loss, and half of them friends and neighbors, getting up an hour earlier each day to make sure there was a *minyan* so that the mourners' prayers could be properly said.

Following the interment, the family observes

shiva, the week of mourning (*shiva* means "seven," as in "seven days"), interrupted only by the Sabbath. They put all worldly concerns aside and stay home to concentrate on their loss and begin to heal. Friends come to visit them and talk about the deceased. In a lovely symbolic custom, the bereaved do not prepare their own meals during *shiva* but are fed by others, as if to recognize that they are empty and need to be replenished by the community.

Because the subject of death makes us all anxious, many people don't know how to pay a condolence call. They have the idea that they serve the mourners' needs by changing the subject, talking about the weather, the stock market, or recipes rather than about the person who has just died. But the mourner needs to talk about his or her loss. When I have had a loss and observed the week of *shiva,* the callers I appreciated most were the ones who told me something of their encounters with the one who had just died, sharing anecdotes and perspectives about that person I might not have known about.

I generally advise people that, if you cannot do both and have to choose between attending the funeral and paying a condolence call, you help the bereaved more by the condolence call. You don't have to be concerned about what to say, as if the admission ticket for such a visit was a comment so profound that it could cure grief. Simply say, "I'm sorry," and if you didn't know the deceased, say, "Tell me about your mother; what was she like?"

One more piece of advice: Chances are that the average family in mourning has more flowers, fruit baskets, and casseroles than they can handle, well intentioned though the offering may be. If you are a close friend, ask what you can do for them (carpooling the children to music lessons or Religious School classes may be more helpful than sending flowers). Otherwise, a contribution to your or their favorite charity is an appropriate way of saying that you care, and letting the memory of the deceased endure as a blessing.

Perhaps the single most prominent and consistent theme of this book has been Judaism's focus on sanctifying the ordinary, spotlighting the specialness hidden in the most commonplace events. Statistically, birth and death are everyday occurrences. Millions of people are born every day, and millions of other people die. Statistically, there is nothing unusual about people getting married. But when it is our parent who has died, our child born, our daughter married, we know that something special, something out-of-the-ordinary is happening. We ask our religious tradition to teach us how to transcend the statistics, how to redeem the moment from the realm of the ordinary. We ask it to teach us that the story of two people committing themselves to love each other is a masterpiece that God has wrought, and not just a matter of maintaining the species. We ask it to remind us that the death of a good person significantly diminishes God's world, and that the birth of a Jewish child, and that child's growing up to affirm his or her Jewish heritage, strengthens God's presence in the world. We ask Judaism to help us celebrate the fact that a Bar Mitzvah is more than a birthday party, a wedding is more than a legal agreement. We ask Judaism to help us respond to death as more than a biological event. We want it to give us the words to say, to tell us what to do, and to know that we are doing what generations of Jews before us have done at just such moments in their own lives. And Judaism responds by giving us what we need.

9

Why We Love Israel

I PULL INTO the parking lot at two minutes after the hour, arriving a bit late for my meeting but confident that the others will be even later. The station on my car radio has just gone to its hourly news summary. I reach to turn off the radio and the ignition when the announcer says, "And in the Middle East . . .," and I stay my hand and sit in the car listening. Why do I do that? Why do I fasten on every bit of news from Israel with such intensity, feeling as I do so a little like my grandmother, who would scan lists of airplane crash victims looking for Jewish names.

Over the years, I have found that the issue that puzzles non-Jews the most about Judaism is the role that Israel plays in our minds and souls. It has no analogue in the Christian world. It cannot be compared to the Catholic's feelings toward the Vatican, or the Lutheran's to Germany. It is different from the emotional attachment of Italian-Americans to Italy or Irish-Americans to Ireland. The ancestors of most American Jews came from

Europe, not Israel. Few of us can trace our ancestry back far enough to identify a forebear who lived in the Middle East.

Moreover, the attachment is emotional, not nostalgic or theological. It cuts across all religious and social borders. Religious and nonreligious Jews, orthodox and liberal, rich and poor are more united by their love for Israel than by any other single subject on the Jewish agenda (except perhaps for antisemitism). How shall we understand this?

The attachment is not political. Every Jew I know makes a distinction between the idea of a Jewish homeland in Israel (to which we are passionately and wholeheartedly committed) and the political state of Israel (of whose government we may or may not approve—not that different from most Americans who are totally committed to the idea of America as a democracy but may think that the policies of a current president are misguided). American Jews are citizens of only one country, the United States.

Neither is the attachment religious; nonreligious Jews feel as strongly about Israel as do our more religious neighbors. (For many of them, love of Israel virtually *is* their religion.) Nor is it exactly historical; statistically, more Jewish history has happened outside Israel than within its borders, from the giving of the Torah in the Sinai desert to the codifying of the Talmud in Babylonia to the philosophical writings of Maimonides in Spain and the insights of Freud and Einstein in Europe.

What, then, is the nature of this attachment? Partly, our love for Israel, like all love, is irrational and does not lend itself to being explained and understood. But parts of it, I think we can understand.

When God and Israel entered into a Covenant at Sinai, God asked the people to live a distinctive lifestyle, to be a model nation, and the people promised that they would. What was God's part of the Covenant? What did He promise in return? Not a life of ease and splendor. God's promise was, first, a sense of His presence, the feeling that we were a unique, special people, and, second, that we would have *a land of our own.* And later in the Bible, when the prophets want to threaten Israel with the worst fate imaginable as a punishment for faithlessness, what do they say? They warn Israel that God will withdraw His presence from them and make them ordinary, and that they will be driven out of their land.

Israel symbolizes for us the idea that we are a people, not only a belief system. It has been one of the recurrent themes of this book that Judaism is rooted more in community than in theology. A theology can exist in the pages of a book. It can be adhered to by individuals wherever they may live, and those individuals may choose to gather in a church from time to time to affirm their solidarity. But a people is not an abstraction; a people has to live somewhere. Marriage as a legal concept can be confined to the pages of the law codes, but when a man and a woman get married, they have to find a home and furnish it.

We relate to Israel in such a complicated fashion in part because the notion of Israel overlaps several otherwise distinct ideas. On the one hand, Israel is a state, a political entity, with a Jewish majority but a significant Moslem and Christian population and representatives of other religions as well. (Israel contains one of the major shrines of the Baha'i faith and has welcomed a number of Southeast Asian Buddhist refugees.) But at the same time Israel is the homeland of the Jewish people, even those who do not live there and are uncompromised citizens of another country. The blue and white flag with the six-pointed star on it, the anthem *"Hatikvah"* (The Hope), are the flag and anthem of the state of Israel but also the flag and anthem of the Jewish people worldwide. They have a Jewish-religious significance as well as an Israeli-political one. When a Jewish organization opens or concludes a meeting singing *"Hatikvah,"* it is as members of the Jewish people, not as citizens of Israel, that they do so. (Had the state of Israel chosen as its national anthem the 137th Psalm—"By the waters of Babylon we sat down and wept when we remembered Zion. . . . If I forget thee, O Jerusalem . . ."—the psalm would still have been a religious poem and a page from Scripture even while serving as the anthem of a political entity.)

In traditional Jewish sources, the term *Israel* is used interchangeably for the land and for the people. When I officiate at a wedding, the ceremony calls for the groom to say to the bride, "Be thou consecrated unto me by this ring as my wife, according to the laws of Moses and Israel," that is, the Jewish people, the children of Israel. To avoid confusion on the part of the congregation, lest they think that Jewish weddings follow the laws of the state of Israel rather than the Commonwealth of Massachusetts, I instruct the groom to say, ". . . according to the law of Moses and the Jewish people."

Beyond that, the existence of the Jewish state of Israel is an expression of the world's willingness to let the Jewish people live. It is nearly impossible for non-Jews to appreciate the meaning of the scar that the Holocaust, and the centuries of persecution leading up to it, have left on the Jewish soul. I don't know of any other people that wakes up virtually on a daily basis wondering if the world will let them live. Perhaps

African-Americans, perhaps members of other oppressed minorities share this sense of vulnerability. But after the Nazi experience, Jews understand that no matter how economically successful or socially integrated we are, we can never feel totally secure. Even as I write this, the newspapers carry reports of prominent politicians expressing opinions verging on the anti-semitic, of sick minds denying that the Holocaust ever happened, of synagogues being vandalized and skinheads threatening violence against Jews and others whom they dislike. When the children in my congregation would hear about such things and be frightened, I would try to reassure them that there are sick and mixed-up people in all countries, but in America, unlike Nazi Germany, the government and the police are on our side and are working to protect us. International acceptance of Israel delivers that same message on an adult, global level. It says to us, "Despite the haters and the sick minds out there, there is a place for the Jewish people in the world."

This, I suspect, is why so many of us react so defensively when Israel is criticized: because we are always afraid that criticism will lead to a withdrawal of approval of Israel's right to exist at all. It is not paranoia on our part to note the disproportionate amount of energy the United Nations puts into judging Israel. It is not hypersensitivity on our part to notice that no other country is called on continually to justify its right to exist. (Does anyone call for the dismantling of Pakistan and giving the land back to the tens of millions of Hindus who were displaced when a Moslem state was created there in 1947?) There can certainly be valid criticism of the actions and policies of modern Israel; I have engaged in no small amount of it myself. But because of its symbolic importance to us, we become sensitive to the difference between saying, "Israel is not perfect; it should be pressed to improve," and saying, "Israel is not perfect; therefore it should not be protected against its enemies, it should be taken away from its Jewish inhabitants and given to others." The first is geopolitical commentary; the latter is antisemitism, punishing the Jewish state for things that other states would not be held accountable for.

Israel is important to us as American Jews (and again, this will seem strange to someone who has not lived with the feeling of being a cultural minority) because it is the one place where being Jewish is normal, not exceptional. I have heard so many members of my congregation describe this response when they visited Israel, how unexpectedly important and comforting it was for them to realize that everyone around them—the policeman, the taxi driver, the fruit peddler—was Jewish. The early Zionist movement was torn between those who said, "We need a homeland of our own so that we will be free to be the special people that God has summoned us to be," and those who said, "We need a homeland of our own so that we can be a normal people like the Romanians and the Norwegians." Israel attracts some people today because it lets them blend into society rather than stand apart from it. The whole society around them shuts down on the Sabbath and the holy days. They are not bombarded every December with daily reminders that they are different from their neighbors. But for others, Israel offers the possibility of being different, of answering the questions "What kind of society would Jews create if they had a free hand? What would a Jewish educational system look like? A Jewish penal system? A Jewish army?" In a short story that was popular in Israel some years ago, a character refuses to study Jewish history, claiming, "There is no such thing as Jewish history. History is the account of what people do. Jewish history is all about what others do to us." For many of us, the emergence of Israel represents the reentry of the Jewish people into history, the reappropriation of the right to *have* a history, as we did in biblical times, rather than playing a supporting role in other people's history.

I sometimes think that we love Israel for another important reason as well. It has changed our public image, the stereotype that many gentiles call to mind when Jews are mentioned. When I became Bar Mitzvah in 1948, one of the presents I received was a book titled *The Jew in American Sports*. It included biographies of Sid Luckman, Hank Greenberg, the boxer Barney Ross, and an assortment of undistinguished athletes of Jewish origin, to make the point that Jews could be good at physical pursuits. I got a second book about Jews who had been decorated for valor in the Second World War. It was called, I am embarrassed to remember, *Jews Fought Too*. Books like that were written because the public image of the Jew was that of a person who was good at studying and making money but not at anything requiring physical prowess or courage. (An Anglo-Jewish newspaper that carries a weekly sports column once had an article on Jews in the National Football League. All the Jews mentioned in the article were team *owners*.)

Israel changed that. If I were an Israeli, I might prefer my country to have the world's third-strongest economy rather than the world's third-best air force. But as an American Jew, there is something satisfying (in a way, almost too satisfying; have I bought into non-Jewish concepts of what is admirable?) about the Jew as

Israeli soldier or fighter pilot, not only as professor or clothing store merchant, the Jew as Paul Newman in *Exodus* rather than as Woody Allen in *Annie Hall.*

And yet another reason for the major role that Israel plays in the Jewish psyche. By going back to the ancient homeland, we identify ourselves as the descendants of the people who gave the world the Bible. Statistically, Jews have lived longer outside Israel than within its borders. But just as some days shape our lives more than others, some centuries shape the self-perception of a people more than others do. It was when we lived in the land of Israel, built a Temple in Jerusalem, wrote the psalms, and heard the prophets, that we became who we are.

That is why archaeology is the hobby of half the population of Israel. To find a fragment of pottery from biblical times, to find a coin from the years of the revolt against Rome, is to prove the continuity of today's Israel with the Israel of biblical times. It verifies the assertion that Israel is not a new, forty-year-old country, but is in fact one of the oldest countries in the world, one of the few places where the same people are living in the same place and speaking the same language as two thousand years ago.

That explains why Jews were moved to tears in June 1967 when the Old City of Jerusalem, the

Western Wall of the Temple, the Tomb of the Patriarchs in Hebron, and other biblical sites became part of Israel. It connected them to their biblical origins, and even nonreligious Jews were thrilled by that. Within two months of the end of the Six-Day War, fully half the population of Israel, most of them nonreligious Jews, had come to Jerusalem to pray at the Western Wall.

A few miles southeast of Jerusalem, on the road to Bethlehem, stands a building known as Rachel's Tomb. Tourists are told that this is where Jacob's beloved wife Rachel was buried after dying in childbirth (Genesis 35:19-20). For nineteen years, that religious site was inaccessible to Jews (not only to Israelis or to Zionists, but to any Jew). Then, in 1967, as the Israeli army advanced on Bethlehem and reached Rachel's Tomb, the first thing they saw was the inscription on one wall of the building, words taken from God's promise to Rachel in the thirty-first chapter of Jeremiah, "and your children shall return to their own land."

There is one phrase that has the power to generate more anxiety in the hearts of Jews who love Israel than any other. It is the phrase "dual loyalty," the accusation that we, as American Jews, put the needs of Israel ahead of the needs of the United States. At the most basic level, it is simply not true. American

Jews are loyal Americans and have proven that repeatedly.

But at a more complex level, I would plead guilty to the charge of having multiple loyalties. Indeed, I would claim that it is a poor person who has only one cause to be loyal to. We all have many loyalties—to our families, to our faith, to our job, as well as to our country—and sometimes those loyalties come into conflict. A farmer may urge his congressman to support higher prices for food, a Detroit autoworker or Cleveland steelworker may urge Washington to protect his company against cheaper prices from foreign competitors, even though that will result in food and cars costing more. I am sure that the fundamentalist Christian who says, "I don't care what the Supreme Court says; I'm going to insist on prayer in the public school classroom," doesn't think of himself as putting the interests of his religion above the interests of the United States as a whole. And it should never occur to us that we are less than loyal Americans when we urge our government to support Israel as a beleaguered outpost of democracy and a loyal friend.

Like you, I have many loyalties and am often called on to sort them out when they conflict, as they inevitably do. Sometimes the conflicts are trivial, as when my commitment to good health collides with my being served a tempting dessert, or when my obligation to attend synagogue conflicts with a World Series game. Sometimes the conflicts are more serious. But my primary loyalty is to God and to a sense of my own integrity as a child of God. I feel that I am being a good American and a good Jew when I urge American support for Israel. If I ever felt that I could no longer support Israel without violating my own integrity, I would have to reconsider that support (even as I would have to question my continuing loyalty to a family member if I thought that such loyalty—for example, hiding evidence of a serious crime—violated my integrity). And if the United States should ever change so that I could no longer comfortably be loyal to it, if some future government would endorse a program of racial or religious persecution, I would hope I would have the courage to oppose it, as a handful of brave Germans did during the Hitler years. The British novelist E. M. Forster once wrote that if he had to choose between betraying his country and betraying his friends, he hoped he would have the courage to betray his country. When I first read that statement, I was shocked. It sounded like an endorsement of treason. But the more I thought about it, the more I realized he was saying something much more thoughtful than that. Weren't we, as Americans, horrified and revolted by accounts of Nazi and Communist governments urging children to inform on their parents, to tell the authorities if their parents criticized the government or listened to forbidden radio stations? On those rare occasions when religion and patriotism come into conflict with each other, I don't automatically side with one or with the other. I ask myself, Which alternative permits me to be me and to serve God best?

Do Jews care more about other Jews than they do about non-Jews? I would hope so. When I read the words of the great philosopher Immanuel Kant, that it is philosophically unacceptable for a person to be nicer to his friend than to a stranger, I consider that one of the dumbest things that brilliant man ever said. There is apparently no room in his philosophy for love and loyalty; they are irrational feelings. I don't think my wife would be pleased if I announced that for reasons of philosophical consistency, I decided to love her and all other women in the world equally well. Caring about Jews is not a substitute for caring about people in general. It is a preparation for it.

Sociologist Leonard Fein puts it this way: The brotherhood of Man is too big a concept for me to accept. I can't handle the idea of having five billion brothers. So, says Fein, *I believe in the brotherhood of Jews and the cousinhood of Man.* By being concerned with all Jews, including Jews I have never met and might not like if I did meet, by acknowledging that I owe them my concern because of our shared Jewishness, I learn to care about people I don't know. I practice the habit of loving strangers on my fellow Jews, and when I have perfected it, I will be ready to extend that habit to non-Jewish strangers as well. The proof of the validity of Fein's thesis is that the same Jews who are generous to Israel and to Jewish charitable causes are also the most generous supporters of the United Way, medical research, and museums. As long as Israel remains Israel and America remains America, I will continue to love and to be loyal to both, and to my family, my friends, my synagogue, my community, and my job. And I will believe that I am being a better American for it.

10

Why Do Some People Hate Us?

*T*WO MEMORIES from my years as a rabbi: The first is of a young couple who came to see me because they were in love. They seemed to prove the theory that opposites attract. He was Jewish, dark-haired, and intense; she was blond, calm, and came from a generic midwestern "Protestant-because-that's-what-everybody-in-town-was" background. They wanted to get married, and had decided that she would convert to Judaism so that there would be a single, shared religion in their home and family. I spoke to them about the required period of study that would be involved, and about the ceremony of conversion. I told her that in the eyes of Judaism, she did not have to become Jewish to be a good person, but that we recognized the validity of their wanting their home to be religiously united. I explained to her that becoming Jewish involved joining a world-wide family and not just accepting a theology. And then, as I do with all prospective converts, I told them that there was one more thing they had to be aware of. I told the young woman that there were people out there who had nothing against her today, but who would hate her and her children if she and they were Jewish. I told her that there were not that many of them, and they did not have the support of the government as antisemites have had in some countries, but you never knew when they could make life unpleasant. As I spoke, I could see the young man wince as he remembered the stories of Jewish suffering he had learned in Hebrew School, and as he realized he might be imposing such suffering on the woman he loved. I could see the young woman's eyes cloud over with sadness at the thought of what she might be imposing on her unborn children, perhaps even with embarrassment at the thought of what her fellow Christians had done to the descendants of the people God had loved first.

Second memory: A group of us were sitting over coffee and cake in one family's living room. We were all Jewish, members of the congregation I was then serving, and we all had young children. In the midst of the conversation about local and national politics, one of the wives asked, "If a Nazi-style government were to come to power in the United States, how many of us know a Christian family we would trust to hide our children?" What I remember about that conversation is not that some of us had close Christian friends and others didn't, but that *nobody in that room thought it was a ridiculous question.* Nobody expected it to happen, but nobody considered the possibility unimaginable. That is the extent of the scar that centuries of antisemitism have left on the Jewish soul.

To be a Jew is to grow up with some very painful memories of how the non-Jewish world has treated us. I have met middle-aged Jews who know very little of Jewish history and belief, but have personal memories of having to go home from school through a gauntlet of insults and fistfights, and of companies that would not hire them because they were Jewish. And only recently, one of America's leading golfers resigned from the country club where he had first learned the game, because they refused membership to his Jewish father-in-law.

The issue of antisemitism raises three questions:

—Why do people hate?
—Why have we Jews traditionally been the targets of such hatred?
—What can we as Jews do about it?

As to why people hate, and why they hate

Jews, let me state emphatically that antisemitism is not caused by Jewish misbehavior and will not be eliminated by our changing the way we behave. If some Jews are loud and aggressive or guilty of unethical business practices (as are lots of gentiles), one is entitled to dislike them as individuals but has no right to extend that dislike to innocent members of a larger group. Antisemitism, like all racial and religious prejudice, is a sign that *something is wrong with the hater, not with his victim.*

I once heard a sermon on the passage in Genesis 29:31 "And the Lord saw that Leah was hated" by her husband Jacob. You may remember the story. Jacob had got into trouble at home by presenting himself to his blind father Isaac as his older brother Esau and getting the blessing of the firstborn by deceitful means. He had to run away to the home of his uncle Laban in Syria, where he fell in love with Laban's beautiful younger daughter, Rachel. Not having money for a bride-price, he worked seven years for the right to marry Rachel. But amidst the drinking and merrymaking of the wedding night, Laban substituted his unattractive older daughter, Leah, for Rachel. Jacob had to work an additional seven years for Rachel. The speaker that morning said, "I can understand that Jacob would hate Laban for cheating him. I can understand that he would love Rachel more than he loved Leah, that perhaps he would not love Leah at all. But why does he *hate* Leah?" His answer: Jacob hates Leah because she reminds him of something he hates in himself, the time he substituted himself for his brother and deceived his father. Every time he sees Leah, he is reminded of that shameful moment. When Jacob complains to Laban about the deceit, Laban justifies it by saying, "It is not right to let the younger one go ahead of the older," which of course is precisely what Jacob had done.

We hate people because they remind us of something we hate about ourselves. Psychoanalysts like Carl Jung and Erik Erikson have defined the concept of the Other, a person very different from us in race, religion, or gender whom we see as embodying all the things we don't want to admit to being ourselves. If we are tempted to be dishonest in business or family matters, we make ourselves feel better by saying, "I'm not a dishonest person. Jews or blacks [or some other vulnerable minority] are dishonest, and since I'm obviously not black [or whatever], I must be all right. I'm not a problem drinker. Only Irishmen are problem drinkers and I'm not Irish." Because these stereotypes have nothing to do with reality, but have a lot to do with our bad feelings about ourselves, they can be wildly unrealistic and self-contradictory, seeing the Other, the person we don't like, as being oversexed and impotent, weak and dangerously powerful, pushy and clannish, at the same time. We can have these contradictory images of people we hate because we are not really describing them. We are projecting on to them qualities we don't want to have associated with ourselves. And then, of course, we have to work very hard at not learning that blacks or Hispanics or Roman Catholics are really a lot like us.

People hate, then, because they are small-souled, insecure, emotionally flawed people. In many cases, they hate themselves first and have to convince themselves that other people are even worse. Because people like that need the ministrations of religion to help them deal with their feelings of badness, they are very often attracted to the church or synagogue. This may explain why religions preach love but ostensibly religious people don't always practice it. I have often said, responding to criticisms of the behavior of prominent synagogue members, that a church or synagogue that accepted only saints as members would be like a hospital that admitted only healthy people. It would be a lot easier to run, but that is not what we are here for.

Fear and envy may also play a role. We teach people in America that anything is possible if you work hard enough at it, but when people different from us start to work hard, we panic at the competition. Look at how quickly our attitude toward minorities—Asian-American college students, black athletes, Japanese automobile makers—changes from "Keep them out, they're not good enough," to "Keep them out, they're taking over."

But why have some people in every century fastened on the Jews as objects of their bigotry? Since antisemitism seems to be the "common cold" of prejudices, the explanations for it are numerous.

First, we Jews are a minority virtually everywhere we live, and, as a minority, are vulnerable to being stigmatized as the Other. Where most people in a society identify themselves as Christians, "non-Christian" can be taken as a synonym for "bad," "deficient." But this can be only a limited explanation. There are other religions and ethnic minorities that have been mistreated but not as virulently or consistently as we have. And more remarkably, there have been antisemitic tendencies even in countries where no Jews lived, such as sixteenth-century England—Shakespeare had never met a Jew when he created Shylock—or twentieth-century Saudi Arabia!

Some historians of the phenomenon of antisemitism see the Jew as the source of conscience, and see the world as resenting us for that. As the writer Maurice Samuel put it, "Nobody loves his alarm clock." We may take pride in the fact that it was to the Jews that God first proclaimed that it was wrong (not merely illegal) to steal, kill, or commit adultery. But other people resent us for telling them that, even as they resent the doctor who tells them to cut out desserts or the policeman who prevents them from speeding. People don't like to be told "Thou shalt not."

I suspect that much of the eagerness of Western governments and liberal Christians to criticize Israel is motivated by resentment of Jewish moral superiority in the aftermath of the Holocaust. Faced with the legacy of a situation where Christians were villains and Jews were innocent victims, many people are desperately eager to be able to say of Jews, "You see, they are no better than we are. When they are in power, they become just like Nazis." This is the paradox of antisemitism. We may be as normal, as imperfect as everyone else, but some people can't forget that we taught the world "Thou shalt not." And even when we strive to be a blessing to the world, to be more charitable, more family centered than other people so that the nations will admire us for it, they are just as likely to resent us for our efforts.

In my readings, I have run across another theory as to why the Jews have been the targets of persecution, not only during the Dark Ages of medieval Europe but in the "enlightened" twentieth century as well. Because our tradition teaches us to identify with the oppressed and to take the well-being of this world seriously, and because the status quo was often an unfair and painful one for us, Jews have often been attracted to movements for social change. We remembered the story of the Passover Exodus and supported the American, French, and Russian revolutions against the tyranny of kings. We were in the forefront of the struggle to advance the rights of blacks and women. Having felt the heavy hand of government oppression, we tended to endorse expanded personal freedom and oppose censorship, even when the freedom in question was the freedom to march through Jewish neighborhoods in Nazi uniforms and the material we defended against the censor was material we found offensive. We put the principle of freedom ahead of our own feelings, even ahead of our own self-interest. But not everyone appreciated that. Some people, especially people who are comfortable with the status quo, are afraid of social change. They find it threatening to their status, their power, or their sense of a familiar world. These people see Jews disproportionately active in Socialist causes, in the civil rights movement, in the American Civil Liberties Union, and they brand all Jews as troublemakers and threats to society.

You may be familiar with the Dreyfus trial in France a century ago. Alfred Dreyfus was an assimilated Jew and a career army officer. When a message was intercepted passing military secrets to the Germans, many people were quick to suspect Dreyfus as the traitor. His trial and conviction, on patently false evidence, divided France into two camps. Feelings were so intense that hostesses at dinner parties would begin the evening by insisting that there be no mention of the Dreyfus affair lest the party degenerate into bitter argument. Why were feelings so strong? What was at stake was more than the guilt or innocence of one man. (Ironically, Dreyfus hardly thought of himself as Jewish, though all of France did.) Dreyfus was the symbol of the New France as against the Old, prerevolutionary France. Some Frenchmen welcomed the opening of society to anyone who had something to contribute. Others were nostalgic for the days when the king, the Church, and the army ruled France, and everyone else knew his place and stayed in it (even as some Americans are nostalgic for an era when blacks, Jews, women, and Roman Catholics were content to remain in the shadows and leave the spotlight to "real Americans"). Jews were seen as the agents of the destruction of the Old France and its replacement by a new, less "authentically French" one. When these people looked at someone like Alfred Dreyfus, they saw not just one assimilated Jew who had devoted his life to serving his country. They saw a threat to their traditional way of life, and they hated him for it.

And then, sad to say, there is probably a distinctive Christian element in the tragic history of antisemitism. There have been voices in the Christian community that argued if Christianity is true, Judaism must be false, and vice versa. If Jesus came first to the Jews and (in the Christian view) they rejected him, there must be something perversely blind about them. To these people, for a Hindu not to be a Christian can be explained by ignorance or unfamiliarity, but for a Jew not to accept Christ is willful stubbornness. (Is there an element of insecurity here, of saying, "I have bet my soul that Jesus was the Messiah, and if people who knew him and knew the messianic promises firsthand did not accept him, maybe I am wrong. But I can't face that possibility, so I will persuade myself that they are terribly misguided.")

I was once asked this question at a public lecture: "Doesn't the history of the Jews' wandering and low status prove that they are being cursed for rejecting Jesus?" I answered, "No, not at all, because the people who predicted that the Jews would suffer are the same people who persecuted them. It would be as if I predicted that

that window would break, and then threw a rock through it. That would say more about my propensity for violence than it would about my gift of prophecy."

Unfortunately, the formative centuries of Christianity, the years when the Gospels were written down and the first Church Fathers lived, were a time of intense competition between the emerging Christianity and its parent faith, Judaism. Christianity was trying to show that it was different from, and superior to, Judaism in the eyes of potential Roman converts, and as with advertisers today, they did it by emphasizing the flaws of the competition as well as their own virtues. (Imagine how Coca-Cola drinkers would feel if Pepsi ads were suddenly declared to be infallible Sacred Scripture. Or what would it mean for future historians if our only information about Ronald Reagan's presidency came from Democratic campaign speeches? That is something like what happened when the image of Judaism comes from ancient and medieval Christian documents.)

How do we change people's feelings? How can we teach haters not to hate? We don't do it by changing *our* behavior to make it less provocative, trying to show them what nice people or good citizens we are. There are reasons why Jews should be good neighbors and honest businessmen, but diminishing antisemitism is not one of them. Hatred stems from self-hatred and insecurity within the bigot. That is why it tends to increase in times of economic stress. To the extent that society learns to make fewer people feel left out, to the extent that it offers more economic opportunity and fewer magazine ads featuring the lifestyles of the affluent, leaving the rest of us feeling like failures, fewer Americans will hate their neighbors.

To the extent that America makes it clear that bigotry and hatred are unacceptable, repudiating derogatory nicknames and racial-ethnic jokes, fewer Americans will feel free to hate. Remember, the hater is basically an insecure person. He wants to be accepted, and putting another person down is one of his strategies to gain acceptance. The less acceptable such comments become, the less likely he is to utter them.

Some years ago, a Jewish communal organization ran a fascinating experiment in changing antisemitic attitudes. They went to a summer camp run by the YMCA movement, a camp for Christian teenagers. They administered a psychological test to measure attitudes toward Jews. They then divided the camp into three groups. Group one was given six hours of indoctrination about Jewish contributions to civilization, from the Bible to great artists, athletes, and medical researchers who were Jewish. Group two was exposed to the history of Jewish suffering, how we had been persecuted over the centuries, culminating in the Holocaust, and how nobly we had borne those sufferings. Group three was not taught anything about Judaism. Instead, they spent their six hours talking about how foolish it was to generalize about people, to lump them in groups. At the end of the week, the same psychological test was administered to see if there had been any change in attitude. The first group, the ones who had learned about Jewish contributions to civilization, were unchanged. The group that learned about Jewish suffering showed a slight *increase* in antisemitic attitudes. (Resentment of Jewish claims to moral superiority? Belief that "where there's smoke, there's fire"?) The group in which teenagers told each other that it was dumb to be prejudiced showed a significant *decline* in negative feelings about Jews. Conclusion: We reduce prejudice best by fostering a climate in which it is socially unacceptable to express prejudiced feelings about another group.

What can we do about passages in the New Testament that blame the Jews for the Crucifixion? I cannot ask my Christian neighbor to censor or rewrite his sacred scriptures, any more than feminists or homosexuals can demand that I change the passages in the Torah that offend them. But I *can* ask him to understand those passages in their historical setting (even as I do with sexist, proslavery or antigay verses in the Hebrew Bible), and to interpret them in the light of contemporary Christian teaching. One of the heartening results of Jewish-Christian dialogue at the local and international level has been a series of statements, guidelines, and rewritten textbooks condemning as un-Christian the anti-Jewish stereotypes of the past.

But the question of how we respond to antisemitism has another, more important dimension. Not only must we be concerned with shaping the attitudes of the gentile world around us. How shall *we* deal with this painful heritage of our past? I have some strong opinions on the subject. I think we owe it to the martyrs of the Jewish past to honor their memories and preserve the record of their suffering. Our Jewish heritage is rendered more precious by the sacrifices they made for it. Moreover, the lesson that the world can be a cruel and unfair place is one we need to learn, and one to which we as Jews need to bear witness. But I think it is a serious mistake, for several reasons, to base too much of our perception of Judaism on this bloodstained past.

First, it teaches us to see Judaism in a negative light, as a burden and a source of danger rather than as a blessing and a source of spiritual empowerment. That would be historically untrue. Jews lived happily and productively in Spain for hundreds of years before the Inquisition and the Expulsion of 1492. We created great Jewish communities in Poland and Lithuania over a period of one thousand years before those communities were destroyed by the Nazis. To know nothing about them except their tragic end, to see Jewish history solely in terms of bloodshed and persecution, would be like describing the life of a good and dear friend as a bitter tragedy because toward the end of it, he got sick and died.

But in addition to being historically inaccurate, this emphasis on Jewish suffering is psychologically counterproductive. We may sympathize with people whom we see as life's losers but we will not be eager to join them. When children show up for their Hebrew School lessons and say to each other, "I didn't do the history homework for today; what country do we get kicked out of in this chapter?," we are not teaching them to take pride in the heroism of the Jewish past. When a man says, "I don't take my Judaism too seriously but I'm not about to abandon it when it is under attack by bigots," he is not only making religion marginal to his life. He is setting himself up to give it up entirely as soon as it is no longer besieged.

When we are taught in our study of Jewish

history to think of Jews in their role as victim rather than in their role as bearers of God's light, when courses about the Holocaust are the most popular offerings in college Jewish Studies departments, we learn to think of Judaism in negative terms, a problem to be borne bravely if it can't be solved. Some of the saddest people I know are Jews who tried to run away from their Jewishness—changed their names, underwent cosmetic surgery, told jokes that made fun of Judaism and Jewish rituals—thinking that this would render them less vulnerable to antisemitism. (My teacher Mordecai Kaplan used to say that "expecting the antisemite to like you better because you were a nonobservant Jew was like expecting the bull not to attack you because you were a vegetarian.") They are left with all the costs of being Jewish and none of the benefits.

To base one's Jewish identity on antisemitism is to create a need to find the threat of antisemitism even when it is not there. If our only reason for remaining Jewish is that the gentile world hates and excludes us, what happens if they stop? Will we be so surprised by their acceptance that we win rush delightedly into their embrace? We either have to find evidence of the danger of antisemitism around us or else be tempted to give up our Jewishness in its absence. We end up being Jews only because we have to, not because we wish to. When someone says to me, "Scratch a *goy* and you'll find an antisemite," I'm tempted to say to him, "You know, maybe if you stopped scratching him, he'd have fewer reasons to dislike you."

The nasty little secret is that there is something emotionally satisfying about portraying yourself as a victim. It permits us to claim the moral high ground in an argument, to claim moral superiority over our opponent. It lets us attribute our failures to someone else's prejudice rather than to our own limitations. I have encountered this attitude among divorcées and accident victims who never "get over" what was done to them because "getting over it," returning to normal, would mean no longer having a claim on other people's sympathy.

The third reason for not basing our understanding of what it means to be Jewish on the sufferings of Jews in the remote and recent past is that it distorts our relationship with the people around us. Guilt doesn't bring out the best in anybody. When we confront our Christian neighbors with an attitude of "I'm Jewish, you're Christian; therefore, you owe me one for the Holocaust," they probably won't be moved to apologize sincerely and try to make it up to you. They will probably become resentful and defensive. (How do we respond to people who say to us,

"I'm black, you're white; you owe me something for those generations of slavery"?)

I don't want my neighbor to love me or to feel sorry for me because some Christian he never met sent some Jew I never met to the gas chambers of Auschwitz, any more than I would accept his disliking me and my children because some Jew I don't know cheated him in a business deal. If the nations of the Christian West voted to establish Israel in 1947 because they felt guilty for what happened in the Holocaust, I'll take it. But I would rather have them recognize Israel, not out of guilt but out of the recognition that we Jews are a people and a people needs a place to live. If support for Israel is based on guilt, it will engender resentment and ultimately lead to a withdrawal of support when time causes those guilt feelings to fade.

I would hope that fifty years from now, a book about Judaism would not have to include a chapter on antisemitism (unless it was a book on Jewish history). In the meantime, I expect my government to protect me from being harmed or harassed by antisemites. I expect the organized Jewish community to work to diminish antisemitism and all forms of racial and religious prejudice. But I don't want anybody to feel sorry for me because I'm Jewish. To me, being Jewish is something wonderful. It is an immense privilege given to only one person out of every three hundred in the world. The attraction of a life of blessing, not the fear of rejection at the hands of bigots, drives my sense of Jewish identity. I can dimly understand why insecure, small-souled people persecuted my ancestors in Europe for being Jewish. I can understand much more clearly why my ancestors thought being Jewish was important and worthwhile enough to endure that persecution.

11

Jews and Christians in Today's World

CHRISTIANS need to understand Judaism theologically, even if they never meet a live Jew. They need to understand what God had in mind when He entered into a Covenant with the Jewish people, and how that was changed by the birth and death of Jesus. Jews don't need to understand Christianity theologically, but we need to understand it practically, sociologically. We need to figure out what it means to live as Jews in a society where 90 percent of our neighbors are Christians, basing their religion partly on Hebrew Scriptures and partly on texts and traditions that go beyond them.

How shall we understand Christianity? How shall we regard Jesus, who was born a Jew and is now regarded as the Divine Savior, Son of God, by so many of our neighbors? And how shall we understand the historical developments that saw Christianity begin as a tiny sect within Judaism and go on to become the religion of half the world? If we worship the same God and revere the same Bible, why are so many people sitting in their section of the bleachers and so few in ours?

Let me emphasize that this chapter is not a scholarly history of Christianity or an introduction to its theology. Neither is it an attempt to suggest to a Christian reader of this book that his beliefs may be wrong. It is a Jewish perspective on the phenomenon of Christianity emerging from Jewish roots.

We begin with the historical setting in which Christianity arose. What we now think of as the first century of the Christian era, the century in which Jesus lived and died, was a time of messianic ferment in the Roman province of Judea. In biblical times, that land had been called Israel. It would later be called Palestine, as the Romans tried to erase the memory of a Jewish presence by naming it after a seafaring Mediterranean people who had briefly inhabited the coast around 1100 B.C. Since 1948, it has been called Israel again. The Roman rulers were cruel and greedy, collecting outrageous sums in taxes to finance their empire and putting to death anyone suspected of being a potential troublemaker. Times were so hard that people believed God would imminently intervene to save them as He had in Egypt. They compared the pain of their situation to the travail of a woman giving birth; the pains are most intense just before delivery. They not only prayed for a messianic redeemer; they expected his arrival daily.

The Hebrew word *Messiah* was originally a synonym for the king. The word means "king," the one who was crowned by having the anointing oil poured on his head. (It literally means "the anointed one," as does the Greek *christos*.) In biblical times, the Messiah for whom the people prayed was a just and honest king, more decent and effective than the one currently ruling them. Like all legitimate kings of Israel, he would be a descendant of King David, but he was not seen as having any superhuman powers. The prophet Isaiah describes him this way:

There shall come forth a shoot from the stump of Jesse [David's father],
    and a branch shall grow out of its roots.
    And the spirit of the Lord shall be upon him,
    the spirit of wisdom and understanding,
    the spirit of counsel and might,
    the spirit of knowledge and the fear of the Lord.
    He shall not judge by what his eyes see,
    or decide by what his ears hear.
    With righteousness shall he judge the poor,
    and decide with equity for the meek of the earth. [Isaiah 11:1–4]

*   *   *

In other words, if we could just have a good, honest, inspired king, he would solve all our problems.

Eight hundred years after Isaiah spoke, the land of the Jews, like most of Europe and the Middle East, had become part of the Roman Empire. Now it was not enough to hope for a fair and honest ruler. Before a Jewish king could begin judging the poor righteously, he first had to chase away the Roman occupier, and that would require divine intervention on a miraculous scale. Now the Messiah had to be a superhuman figure—not the Son of God or the Redeemer from Sin (those are non-Jewish concepts introduced by early Christianity), but a person capable of leading the Jews to victory over the greatest military force in the world.

It was into this setting that Jesus of Nazareth was born. We don't know anything for certain about his life. All we know about him comes from accounts written two generations later by people who believed that he was the Messiah and wanted to persuade others of that fact. But the following seems to be a plausible outline of his career:

He was born into a working-class family in Nazareth, a rural city in the Galilee in northern Israel, far from the centers of learning and political power. Later Christian sources would add an account of his parents traveling to Bethlehem when he was due to be born, because Bethlehem was King David's hometown and there was a tradition that the Messiah would come from there. But many Jewish and Christian scholars doubt that.

The young man (whose Hebrew name meant "God will save") grew up to be a compelling and charismatic teacher and preacher, offering a view of Judaism (shared with many of the leading Jewish teachers of that time) that emphasized inward perfection more than external performance. Albert Schweitzer has suggested that the central idea in Jesus' teaching was the conviction that the world was going to end very soon, probably in his lifetime. Everyone, therefore, needed to put aside all other concerns (getting married, earning a living) and prepare for the End of Days and the Judgment. That is why he preached an ethic (turn the other cheek, don't hate or covet, don't worry about your parents or family) that people might be able to follow in the short run but not for a lifetime.

Many people responded to his message and his effective way of presenting it, and he began to develop a reputation and a following. Because he had this gift of making people want to follow him and do what he asked them to do, some people began to wonder if he might be the heaven-sent redeemer.

What follows is a personal, somewhat unconventional but plausible interpretation of the Gospel accounts in the New Testament. One day, someone asked him, "Master, shall we pay our taxes to Rome?" In other words, "Shall we rise in revolt?" Stopping the flow of taxes was the traditional way of beginning a revolt. Jesus held up a coin and asked, "Whose likeness is on this coin?" "Caesar's," the people answered. "Then render unto Caesar what is Caesar's, and unto God what is God's." That is, pay your taxes; the revolution I have come to call for is a spiritual one, not a political one. In the next verse (Matthew 22:22), "When they heard these words, they marvelled and left him and went on their way." I take that to mean that they were disappointed that he did not promise to expel the Romans, and stopped following him.

Shortly after that, Jesus and a few disciples made their way to Jerusalem for Passover. As we remember from our discussion of the pilgrim festivals, every Jew who was physically able to do so would travel to Jerusalem to celebrate Passover at the Temple. I can imagine that this made the Roman authorities nervous. First of all, the streets were crowded with tens of thousands of pilgrims who might easily become an uncontrollable mob. Second, the message of Passover, a message of divinely assisted liberation, was likely to inspire some hotheaded Jews to rise in revolt. I can believe that the Roman authorities adopted a policy of "crack down first and investigate later."

Jesus celebrated what has become known as the Last Supper (it may or may not have been a Passover Seder) with a dozen of his followers, and after that was arrested and brought before the High Priest and the elders of the Jewish community. The New Testament account, written years later and slanted to impress a Roman audience, tells of the Jewish authorities convicting him of blasphemy and turning him over to the Romans for punishment. But I am attracted to the theory of Israeli Supreme Court Justice Haim Cohen, who suggests that Jesus was brought before the Jewish authorities not to judge him or condemn him (Jewish courts did not meet at night or on the eve of holidays, and if the Last Supper was a Seder, it is inconceivable that the Jewish court would meet on Passover) but to *warn* him. Here was this popular, gifted young Jewish teacher from a small town in the Galilee who did not realize what a dangerous place Jerusalem was at Passover time. Make yourself too conspicuous, I can picture the elders telling him, attract large crowds, and the Romans will see you as a potential troublemaker.

A day or two later, Jesus was put to death by

crucifixion, a particularly cruel form of execution. It is very clear from all accounts that he was killed by the Romans, not by Jews, and that he was one of many people crucified by the Romans in Judea. After his death, his closest friends and followers began to see visions of him (it is not unusual for people to dream or daydream about someone they loved and lost; it has happened to me) and began to believe that he had risen from the dead and must indeed have been the Messiah. At this point, we begin to move from the religion *of* Jesus (love your neighbor, turn the other cheek, prepare for the End of Days) to the religion *about* Jesus (he was the Son of God who died to absolve us of our sins). The key figure in this shift was a Jew named Paul, known in Christian tradition as Saint Paul, author of many of the books of the New Testament.

Jesus' disciples, all of whom were Jewish, tried to persuade their fellow Jews that the young teacher who had been put to death was the Messiah. They had very little success doing so. Paul, who had never met Jesus but became convinced of his divine mission, found the non-Jewish world more receptive. He brilliantly combined the strenuous moral teachings of the Jewish tradition with familiar elements of pagan religion that had not been part of Jesus' original message—the leader, born of a divine father and human mother, who dies and comes back to life. Perhaps out of conflicts within his own personality, he crafted the very non-Jewish notion of Original Sin, that because none of us is perfect, we are all condemned to hell and only the willing sacrifice of a perfect, sinless man (God come down in human form) can save us.

Within three hundred years, Christianity went from being a handful of individuals within Judaism to being a persecuted sect, to being a tolerated sect, and finally to becoming the official religion of the Roman Empire. Why did Christianity succeed in winning the hearts of tens of millions of people while Judaism, which was an energetically missionary religion at that time, remained the inheritance of a much smaller population? When I was in Hebrew School, I was taught that Christianity was more attractive because it was easier: no dietary laws, no Sabbath observance, no need to circumcise male converts. But it was not that easy to be a Christian in the first or second century. (Remember all those movies where Christians are thrown to the lions to entertain Roman audiences?) Part of the answer lies in the fact that in the year 67 and again in the year 135 (the Bar Kochba rebellion), the Jews rose in revolt against Rome, seeking their freedom. Both times, they fought heroically, and both revolts were put down with great loss of life. The Romans were so angry at having to send troops to put down these revolts that they tried to crush Judaism in Judea, forbidding its teaching or practice. That was when they destroyed the Second Temple and changed the name of Judea to Palestine, and that is why the definitive Talmud, the commentary on how the laws of the Torah were to be lived, was written in Babylonia rather than in Judea. As a result, Judaism was physically and emotionally depleted at home, and had the image of being a nation of losers and troublemakers throughout the empire.

But mostly, the question "Why Christianity rather than Judaism?" is the wrong question. The real question is "Why Christianity rather than paganism?" The people of the Roman Empire did not have to choose between Judaism and Christianity. They had a third option: remaining pagans, worshipping the nature-gods of the old religions. Why did so many of them choose Christianity? Having the emperor designate it the official religion of the empire certainly helped. But I believe that there is something in the human soul that responds to the call to righteousness, the summons to be moral. We intuitively know that we are different from the animals, and that this difference is located in our ability to know right from wrong. We want to believe that our moral choices are taken seriously, and only biblical monotheism, whether in its Jewish or its Christian formulation, offered that message.

How shall we, twentieth-century Jews, regard Jesus and how shall we regard Christianity? To be sure, if we are Jewish, we cannot regard Jesus as having been divine. Jews who accept Jesus as their Savior are not "Jews for Jesus"; they are Christians, in the same way that Christians who convert to Judaism are Jews, not "Christians who deny Christ." We can overlook his Jewish origins and the Jewish roots of much that he taught, and see Jesus merely as the central figure of someone else's religion, as we see Mohammed, Confucius, and the Buddha. But my position would be to see Jesus and Paul as people used by God to bring the monotheism and the moral message of Judaism to the world, and to teach the world that the God discovered and worshipped by the Jews was the only true God.

Earlier in this century there lived a brilliant young German-Jewish scholar named Franz Rosenzweig. He grew up with minimal Jewish knowledge, became involved with Judaism as an adult, and died at a tragically young age, but in a few years produced a life's work of books, essays, and projects. Rosenzweig was loyally Jewish but he recognized the spiritual depth and beauty of Christianity and the saintly lives of many of his Christian friends. He knew too many devout Christians to be able to claim that if one religion is true, the other had to be false. He came up with the "two covenant" theory, a way of affirming the religious validity of both Judaism and Christianity.

Judaism and Christianity, he taught, needed each other, and God's plan for humanity needs them both. Christianity grew to be a religion of more than a billion people by absorbing great masses of pagans, sometimes converting entire nations en masse. In the process, these new Christians brought some of their pagan rituals and superstitions into Christianity, diluting its monotheistic message. Adoration of the Virgin Mary sometimes bordered on turning her into a goddess like the mother-goddesses of paganism. Christmas was celebrated with evergreen trees and other winter festival symbols; Easter was observed with eggs, rabbits, and other spring symbols of fertility. Christianity needs Judaism to remind it of what pure, uncompromised ethical monotheism looks like. As a counterpoint to the Christian notion of Original Sin, the idea that no human being can live up to all of God's expectations, Christianity needs the example of the Jewish community actually striving to do what the Torah calls upon us to do.

But Judaism needs Christianity to remind us that the word of God is not meant to be kept for ourselves alone. We are called on not merely to live by God's ways, but to do it in such a manner that the world will be persuaded to turn to God. Had Judaism been as successful in winning converts as Christianity was eighteen hundred years ago, it would have stopped being Judaism. It would have lost the sense of community and shared responsibility that only a small group can maintain. It would inevitably have absorbed many of the superstitions and habits of nature-worship brought by former (and to that point incompletely digested) pagan converts. And yet had the Bible, and the God of the Bible, remained the exclusive property of a few thousand families in and around Jerusalem, God's ultimate plan for the world would have been frustrated. In that way, we Jews can see Christianity as God's chosen instrument for redeeming the world from paganism, and Christians can recognize their obligation to preach the message of Christianity to the world, but *not to the Jewish people,* who had that message before they did.

Significant differences remain, but they are less important than what we share. Some years ago, I was invited to speak to the women's group of the local Methodist Church. The talk was advertised locally, causing one of my congregants to say to me after Sabbath services, "I see you're speaking for the competition Tuesday." I smiled, because I realized he intended his words as a joke, not as a theological statement. But in my mind, my response was "No, Christianity is not the competition. Apathy and selfishness and a neo-paganism that sees Man as an animal and his every urge as legitimate—they are the competition." And the church and the synagogue are allies, on the same side of that battle.

12

Why You Need to Be a Jew

JUDAISM HAS THE POWER to save your life. It can't keep you from dying; no religion can keep a person living forever. (One last Jewish joke: "Rabbi, if I give up drinking, staying up late, and chasing women, and come to your synagogue instead, will that help me live longer?" "No, but it will feel longer.") But Judaism can save your life from being wasted, from being spent on the trivial. I have sat with many people who knew that they were dying. I have held their hands and tried to ease that last passage for them. I have visited people in the hospital late at night to pray with them before they underwent life-or-death surgery the following morning. What they taught me is that people are not afraid of dying; they are afraid of *not having lived*. We don't really want to live forever. (In the words of the British writer G. K. Chesterton, "There are people who pray for eternal life and don't know what to do with themselves on a rainy Sunday.") We want to live long enough to get it right, to know that we have realized our potential and made a difference to the world. Judaism is not just a matter of getting on God's good side by obeying some strange rules He gave us. (I recently read the autobiographical account of an otherwise intelligent young Jew who decided to "test God" by eating a ham sandwich on Yom Kippur. When God didn't strike him down, he concluded that the whole Jewish system was a fraud.) Judaism is a way of making sure that you don't spend your whole life, with its potential for holiness, on eating, sleeping, and paying your bills. It is a guide to investing your life in things that really matter, so that your life will matter. It comes to teach you how to transform pleasure into joy and celebration, how to feel like an extension of God by doing what God does, taking the ordinary and making it holy.

Maybe you have never thought about your Jewishness in these terms before. Maybe someone tried to tell you, but you were too young or too distracted to listen. Or maybe we had to wait until not only you, but the entire American Jewish community, grew up and was ready for this sort of conversation. Rabbi Arthur Hertzberg, in his scholarly history of the Jews in America, has suggested that the Jewish immigration to America was like all immigrations. The poor, the ambitious, those with fewest prospects in the old country were the ones who left home for the new world. The people with money and prestige remained. As a result, the Jews who came to America from Germany in the 1840s and from Russia and Poland in the 1900s tended to be the less learned (learning was a source of prestige in Jewish Europe) and less observant. Many of them harbored resentment against their hometown rabbis for favoring the wealthy over the common Jew. (Think of Tevye in *Fiddler on the Roof* contemplating the prestige he would gain in the synagogue "if [he] were a rich man.") On top of that, the necessity of earning a living in America compelled many Jews to compromise their observance and neglect their prayers and studies. (Hertzberg cites some astonishing statements from East European rabbis urging their followers not to travel to that nonkosher land of America where Jewish life would inevitably be compromised.) Add to that the typical first-generation dynamic where native-born children are embarrassed by the old-country accents and customs of their immigrant parents, and you have a situation where young Jews are not terribly interested in asking questions about their Jewish faith, and their parents are not generally competent to answer them when they do.

For two or three generations, American Judaism consisted largely of an ethnic consciousness and an odd blend of poorly understood rituals and European village folklore, without anyone qualified to distinguish between Jewish law and Polish superstition, and without very much spiritual content. Being Jewish involved food preferences, Bar Mitzvah rituals, an awareness of antisemitism, and (especially after 1967) a determination to support Israel. Hebrew teachers were poorly paid and often poorly trained, but even if they had been better, children got the message that what they learned in synagogue was not important. Public school studies that might lead to a good job were what counted. Like Ulysses' wife Penelope in the *Odyssey,* who would weave a shroud by day and unravel it at night, suburban Jewish parents worked hard at home to undo what the synagogue had tried to accomplish that afternoon. How often did I and my colleagues hear that religious studies must not interfere with public school homework, Little League, or dance lessons. "You know, he doesn't have to be a rabbi!" Where once it was the boast of Judaism that all of its children were learned in the ways of the Lord, the attitude had now emerged that they didn't have to know very much about being Jewish. They could hire someone to know Judaism for them. The effective American Jewish agenda was "work hard to be like everybody else." (I told a friend that I was writing a book on Judaism for everyone who had a bad Hebrew School experience as a child, and he said, "If you do, you'll have a best-seller.")

But human beings cannot live by bread alone. Young Jews raised on a Judaism that was all label and no content began to feel the discomfort of a spiritual vacuum at their core. They were attracted to Buddhism, to the Unification Church, to political and religious fringe movements in an attempt to fill that emptiness. (Why if not in an attempt to satisfy some inner spiritual hunger are Jews 3 percent of the American population and 30 to 40 percent of so many religious and psychological cults?) And recently some of them have even begun to look at traditional Judaism with new seriousness. (If your parents are assimilated Jews, becoming seriously Jewish can be a way of rebelling without rejecting them.) To cite Rabbi Hertzberg again, "A community cannot survive on what it remembers; it will persist only because of what it affirms and believes."

Judaism, done right, has the power to save your life from being spent entirely on the trivial and elevate it to the level of authentic humanity. But it can do more than that. Its goal is not just to make *your* life more satisfying. Its goal is not the survival of the Jewish people. That is a means to an end, not an end in itself. The ultimate goal is to transform the world into the kind of world God had in mind when He created it. Changing your life can affect the lives of people around you, and can create a ripple effect that spreads its influence farther and farther. If that sounds like an audacious claim, remember this: Three thousand years ago, a small band of former slaves came to a new understanding of how human beings were meant to live, how they could change their ways of eating, speaking, and doing business in order to be totally human, and they changed the world forever. People in remote corners of the world are different today because of those moments of ancient revelation.

The Jewish people can still do things like that today. Statistically insignificant as we may be, when we remember who we are, we teach the world lessons about the value of education, the importance of family and community, the obligation of *tzedaka,* the nobility and resiliency of the survivor of persecution, and the potential holiness of the most ordinary of moments. When we remember to utter the message that was entrusted to us, and when the world pauses to listen, we can still change the world.

You may recall from our discussion of the High Holy Days that the Rosh HaShanah prayers often speak of God as King. This has given rise to a genre of stories and parables for Rosh HaShanah picturing God as King and Israel as His first-born son and Crown Prince. In a typical story, the Prince angers the King and is banished from the palace. (You can imagine why these stories were popular in the Middle Ages as a way of putting the Jewish exile in a context.) For years, the King would pine for the son he banished and long to find him. Then one day in the course of his travels, he would come upon his son, now reduced to poverty and begging for bread. In tears, the King would be reconciled to him and invite him back to a place of honor in the palace. A story like that has two morals. One describes God's sorrow over having sent His people into exile, and His longing to be reconciled to them. The other reminds the Jews that we were once entrusted with a special status and mission by God but we have estranged ourselves from Him. We have forgotten that we are the children of the King and worry only about our day-to-day subsistence, while God yearns to reconnect with us and reestablish the relationship.

There is a line in the Book of Isaiah (43:10) in which the prophet pictures God saying to the Jewish people, "You are My witnesses; I am the Lord." In an astonishing comment on those words, the sages say, "When we are His witnesses, He is the Lord. When we neglect being His witnesses, He is not Lord." In other words, God as an abstract concept has little power in the world, but God made real in the lives of people has immense power. Christianity believes that God incarnated Himself, became flesh, in the person of Jesus and changed the world thereby. Judaism teaches that God incarnates Himself in every one of us, and gives us the power to make Him real, not just an abstract notion, in the world, changing the world thereby.

My teacher Mordecai Kaplan has written that some nouns are self-sufficient. Words like *table, chair, knife* need nothing else to be what they are. But some words imply relationship, words like *wife, parent, leader.* You cannot just be a wife; you have to be *somebody's* wife to be a wife. Kaplan suggested that God is such a relational noun. God, to be real, has to be *somebody's* God. He is God in this world only when some people affirm Him and revere Him as God. God without a people to revere Him would be like a parent without a child, a general without an army, a leader without followers. He would be God only in potential. We, by the way we live our lives, make Him God.

But we don't change the world just by remembering that we are Jews; we have to do something about it. Dr. Charles Spezzano writes of students he teaches in medical school who want to *be* doctors but don't want to *do* the actual hard work of studying and practicing medicine. That is, they want the prestige and psychological gratification of the title without the commitment and discipline it inevitably entails. Dr. Spezzano goes on to apply that insight to people who want to *be* married without being willing to *do* marriage. I would make the same point about our Jewish identity. *Being Jewish* is a state of mind; it is something that takes place inside you. It may make you feel proud or it may make you feel uncomfortable, but it remains a private matter. *Doing Jewish* is something that happens between you and other people, between you and the world. Doing Jewish means living differently because you are a Jew.

How does one do Judaism? First, read more books. If you think I included a lot in this book, you'll be surprised to learn how much I left out. Read about Jewish history, Jewish thought and practice. Read Jewish biographies in search of role models.

Find yourself a community. It has been a repeated emphasis of this book that in Judaism, holiness is found in joining with other people, not in fleeing your imperfect neighbors to be alone with God. Search out a synagogue where you will be comfortable, realizing that if it is going to work for you, you have to think of yourself as a part-owner of the synagogue, not just a customer.

Or if you can't find one, get together with a half-dozen other families in search and share your quest with them.

And remember that Jewish commitment is pictured as a *ladder of observance,* not as a leap of faith. You climb a ladder slowly, one step at a time, making sure your footing is secure on one rung before you try the next one. Remember, Jewish tradition imagines God as a teacher, not as an accountant. The issue is not how many *mitzvot* you fulfill, but whether you are learning the elusive art of sanctifying the ordinary moments of your day and week.

If you are part of a family, you might begin with the Friday night rituals of welcoming the Sabbath—lighting candles, blessing the children, *kiddush* over the wine, and a shared meal. You might try the habit of *tzedaka,* or of purifying your speech. You might form the habit of beginning each day with a few moments of prayer—personal meditation, reading from the traditional prayer book or from the Psalms, or attending the *minyan* at your synagogue—just to see if you feel different for having begun your day with an encounter with holiness. Does it make it easier to spread holiness throughout your day? You might want to begin turning your dinner table into an encounter with holiness by selectively and gradually eliminating foods that Jews traditionally avoid (again, not as an effort to please God but as a way of enhancing your humanity by not being utterly casual about eating meat). And throughout it all, remember to say to yourself, to God, and to friends who may be bewildered (and a little threatened) by this new direction your life has taken, "Be patient with me. This is something new and important I'm trying to do, and it may take me a while to get the hang of it."

One of the best-known stories in the Talmud tells of the non-Jew who approached the great sage Hillel and asked him, "Can you summarize all of Judaism for me while I stand on one foot?" Hillel answered, "What you don't like, don't do to others. That's it; the rest is commentary. Now go study the commentary."

Hillel understood that the essence of Judaism was not just a matter of obeying God or pleasing God, as we may have thought (or been taught) when we were children. That is a child's understanding of being good. Nor is the essence of Judaism a matter of escaping this flawed, material world in search of a better, purer one. The essence of Judaism is creating holiness in the way we relate to this world and to the people in it. God cares more about how we treat the poor than how we treat the Torah, and He cares more for how we relate to the rules of the Torah than how we relate to Him.

But Hillel also understood that Judaism is more than its essence, and this is why he told the questioning gentile not to be satisfied with a one-sentence summary, profound as it might be, but to go and study the rest. How we treat our neighbor may have a higher religious priority than how we treat the Torah, but no serious Jew will do one (either one) to the exclusion of the other. It is only by immersing ourselves in Torah, and in what eighty generations of sages have said about the Torah, that we learn what we owe our neighbors. And it is only with regular, repeated exposure to the wisdom and the cleansing power of the Torah that we gain the resolve to do what we know is right.

Yet Hillel's last words—"go and study"—are not the last words on the question of what Judaism asks of us. We should study; Judaism has always insisted that knowledge has the power not only to make people smart but to make them good. Having studied, we should commit ourselves to live differently as a result of what we have learned. And having resolved to live differently, we should then go forth to bless God's world and sanctify it.

About the Author

*H*arold Kushner has been a rabbi for over thirty years. In 1981, he wrote *When Bad Things Happen to Good People* in order to cope with a family tragedy and, to his surprise, found that the nation responded overwhelmingly to the very things he had been teaching his congregation. He is also the author of *Who Needs God* (available in EasyRead Type) and *When All You've Ever Wanted Isn't Enough*, which was awarded the Christopher Medal. Harold Kushner's best-selling books have touched millions of people with their highly personal view of Judaism as the author understands, lives, and teaches it. Harold Kushner was born in Brooklyn, New York, and graduated from Columbia University. He was ordained by and awarded a doctoral degree in Bible from the Jewish Theological Seminary. He has six honorary doctorates.